"IN THOSE DAYS"

by

Eleanor Brettle

ACKNOWLEDGMENTS

First to my granddaughter, Emily, whose explosive reaction to my storytelling made me realise how important it is for children to understand how their forebears had lived.

To my son, David, for encouraging me to write down my memories for my grandchildren to read or eventually to turn it into a book. Without his long hours of transferring my scrappy notes onto his computer, it would never have materialised.

Last, but not least, to Sharon who proofread almost eighty thousand words and then went on to get it published.

Thank you all, I could not have done it without your help.

Chapters: _____ Page

Chapter 1

INTRODUCING MY PARENTS' FAMILIES

My father's father (Grandpa Green) had been a vet in Nottingham. Apparently, he was a very well-known and respected vet. He had done a thesis on horses and was a captain in the Royal Horse Artillery during the First World War.

He first shared a practice in St. James's Street in Nottingham city centre and later moved to Welbeck Terrace, a part of Mansfield Road between Victoria Station and Forest Road. This is where I remember him and my Grannie living and he ran his practice from there. We didn't visit their home very often as my Grannie was almost immobile with arthritis and couldn't cope with a lot of visitors. I remember going there to watch the University Rag procession pass each year. There were hundreds of colourful decorated floats and it was a spectacle not to be missed.

Dad's eldest brother, Uncle Bob, had been working in West Africa but I hardly knew him as he retired to live at Skegness to be near Auntie Doris's mother. Auntie Winnie worked for Boots the Chemists as a pharmacist.

Next came Auntie Madge who married Frank. He worked for Player's (cigarettes) and they lived in London in a hotel, I was told they lived a life of luxury. Dad was next in line and then came Uncle Laurie, who married Florence, who came from Balderton. She was known as Auntie 'Bill'. They were my Godparents and they were great favourites. They lived for many years on the Gold Coast in West Africa as Uncle Laurie was a buyer in the cocoa bean industry. They came home by ship periodically for holidays and always brought me unusual presents. They had such wonderful stories to tell me about their life and home in West Africa and also about travelling home by sea.

Eventually they returned to Britain during the war and settled in Taunton (Somerset) where I visited them on several occasions during my teens and early twenties. Uncle Laurie then worked for NAAFI and they eventually moved to Slough where I spent many more happy times with them. When Uncle retired, they decided to move back to Nottinghamshire and I found them one of the lovely new bungalows being built on Farthingate in Southwell. After they moved here, we spent a lot of time with them and they visited us on the farm frequently.

Next in line came Uncle Harry. He was not so fortunate. Sadly, he was killed in the 1914-18 war as a young man. We found his grave at Bethune in France on our return journey from Oberammergau in 1970. It was in the village cemetery and beautifully kept. His name had been recorded in the Book of Remembrance (there is more information on the internet). He had attended Nottingham High School and his name is on the war memorial there and at St. Andrew's Church.

Auntie Muriel was the youngest of the family and stayed at home to care for her parents. After their death, she and Auntie Winnie moved to Arboretum Street. Soon afterwards, about the middle of the war and during an air raid at night, Mum was reading the Nottingham Evening Post and said to my dad, "Alf, your sister Muriel got married today." She had met and married a farmer named Bill. He lived at Tythby Grange near Bingham, and for the remainder of the war and long after they would bring us home-made pork pies and sausages whenever they killed a pig. We also received new laid eggs and many other goodies. This was a real treat as food was still rationed.

After Mum died in November 1944, Dad and I spent several holidays at Tythby Grange. We went there that Christmas and they made me feel very grown up. It was an enormous farm house and I had never seen such a huge dining table as the one where we all ate our Christmas dinner. I remember drinking sparkling Muscatel from champagne glasses, a first for me.

That was my father's family. He was the middle one of the seven and the only one to have any children. Consequently, we had no cousins on that side.

My mother's father (Grandpa Raynor) was in the lace trade in Nottingham. He and Grannie lived in a big house on Waterloo Crescent near the Forest Recreation Ground. Mum was the eldest of six daughters. When she left school, she became a private governess. She and my dad married in 1923, they had Harry a year later, then Catherine (who died of meningitis at 17 months) and then me.

Dad would have loved to have been a vet, but after serving as a soldier during the 1914-18 war was ready to settle down and he decided to enter the Civil Service and went into the Inland Revenue.

Auntie Hylda was next and married Uncle Arthur who was a director of Turney Brothers, the leather tanning works at Trent Bridge. They had a daughter Joan and lived in a big house on Arboretum Street where they had a maid called May. Joan had a nursery where I loved to play with her. Auntie Hylda died when Joan was nine and Uncle Arthur re-married. Joan was then sent to Penrhos College for Girls Boarding School in North Wales, but was later evacuated to Chatsworth House for the duration of the war.

Auntie Rita was next and she married Uncle Eric. They were only married seven years when he died as a result of a wound received during the Spanish Civil War (see International Brigade).

Auntie Vera was next in line. She remained single. She had stayed at home to care for her parents and after they died in the early 1950's got a job in the

3

Inland Revenue office, where she stayed until her retirement. She and Auntie Rita lived together on Ebers Grove for many years after they left Waterloo Crescent.

Auntie Zena married Uncle Leo and they had my cousin Mary. He worked for Player's (cigarettes) and they lived at Sherwood when Mary was young. She had the most fabulous parties. Auntie Zena loved the theatre and craved for London. So when Uncle had the opportunity to move there, they were gone.

We saw less of them then, however, I did spend two spells staying with them whilst I did my veterinary training in Surrey. At weekends they introduced me to the best shops in London and we spent many an evening at the theatre. Auntie Freida was the youngest of their family. As an adult she preferred to be called 'Freddie'. She married Uncle Edmund just before the war and lived in Putney, London, where he ran a family butcher's shop. When he joined the army, Freddie couldn't tolerate the 'Doodlebugs' that were hitting London whilst living alone, and she moved to Nottingham to be nearer her family.

Somewhere, sometime, she met a wealthy man named Veere. She left Edmund and married Veere. They set up home in a beautiful apartment in Sloane Street, London. I went there once when I was attending a WI meeting at the Albert Hall. They paid for me to stay in the hotel next door and took me out to dinner at the Mirabelle restaurant. I had never been to such an exquisite restaurant before nor have I since. Next day their chauffeur-driven car picked me up after the WI meeting and took me to Harrods where Auntie Freddie was waiting for me. I think it is the only time a uniformed chauffeur has opened a car door for me - and outside Harrods too.

When Veere retired, they moved to a beautiful big country house at Ansty in Sussex which had a huge garden with a swimming pool. Here Veere grew many vegetables and revelled in his grand garden. We visited a couple of times when our boys were young and swam in the pool. When eventually the house and garden became too much to manage, they moved to an apartment on the sea front at Hove, where we visited them on several occasions.

So of Grannie's six girls, three produced children and three didn't. As a result, we only had two cousins, Joan and Mary.

When I was young, children were taken to visit their grandparents. They didn't stay with them without their parents as they tend to nowadays.

Chapter 2

MY EARLIEST MEMORIES

One of my earliest memories is of being given a ride in my pushchair by my brother Harry, five years my senior, who delighted in the steepness of the path from our front gate to the house. If he let go before the bend, he could be fairly sure I would land in a bed of roses. This was a forerunner of the tricks he would play on me in later years.

I had been born in 1929 – a 'replacement' for the baby sister I never knew. Catherine had died from meningitis at the age of 17 months and my

distraught mother had been advised to have another baby as soon as possible. She was herself not in good health, having a very severe form of chronic asthma. Naturally she had been heartbroken at the loss of her baby girl who was just beginning to say a few words. But my mother said it was Catherine who suffered the broken heart as she had been taken into hospital alone and in isolation. The nurses had said that she had cried consistently for her "Mum, Mum, Mum," but in those days parents were not allowed to stay in hospital with their sick baby.

So, though I couldn't possibly have realised it while I was young, I had a commitment to baby Catherine – to try and live life to the full – to enjoy a birthright denied her, but that she had bestowed on me.

We lived in a council house at Sherwood, a suburb of Nottingham, at the bottom of a hill where there was a back garden to play in and beyond that a small allotment where my farther grew the family's vegetables. I loved to watch him dig and sow rows and rows of different kinds of seeds. Then he would cover them and tread down the soil and finally rake over the surface.

He was very methodical and I must have learnt quite a lot watching him in those early days. Not so many years later I was to become a very keen gardener and I have invariably used the methods my dad showed me all those years ago. I would often wander off alone and sit among the cabbages and the beans and talk to the little robin that was so tame that he would sit on my father's spade handle as soon as he finished digging. But one day when I was only three or four, I was discovered exploring nature with the little boy next door – and we weren't looking for caterpillars as I had apparently told my mother. That was the end of my lone forays into the cabbage patch!

Not far away along the edge of the playing fields on Valley Road was a stream called the Day Brook and here at weekends Dad would take us to catch tiddlers and sticklebacks in a jam-jar. What we did with them I'm not sure. I guess we must have put them back? But I do remember bringing home tadpoles from Mee's Pond which was just beyond the stream in the grounds of a derelict house that was held together with a great iron band. In these grounds were all kinds of wildlife but I particularly remember the beautiful blue dragonflies. They were the first I had ever seen. The old house was said to have been haunted and gave the whole place an air of spookiness. I thought my brother was very brave to go and explore inside without an adult – I certainly would not have done. But in later years, during the War, I was to go there with my science teacher to cut nettles as part of the school's war effort. They were hung in bunches on wires to dry inside the haunted house. They would then be used for medicines and perhaps as an addition to beer instead of hops. We even ate them cooked like cabbage. In the 1930s our streets were lit by gas and I can remember the old lamp-lighter coming round about 4 o'clock on a winter's afternoon. He had a long pole with which to switch on and light the gas lamp. Another man who ran up the road in the late afternoon was the newspaper seller shouting, "Post!" Occasionally there would be a Post 'Extra' or 'Special' earlier in the day if there was some piece of news to relate that couldn't wait till evening, such as a Royal birth or death or a riot in parliament.

Then there was the rag and bone man. He would push his wooden two-wheeled cart shouting, "Rag-bone!" or at least that is what it sounded like. There was a knife-grinder too but he probably only came once a year. I remember my brother Harry getting into trouble one day when he had taken lumps of coal from the coal scuttle and placed them all round the dining room, the table being in the middle. His hands and the carpet were black but he insisted that he was only 'playing trains'.

During the summer following my fifth birthday, we moved to a house on a road at the top of the hill, in order to be nearer the school that I was to attend in September and to make it easier for my mother to get to the shops. It was a bigger house with two living rooms and three bedrooms. There was a good piece of garden back and front and beyond the back fence was a large shrubbery, playground and the infant/junior school where I was to spend six very happy years.

In September 1934 I joined the 'baby's' class at the Seely School where we sat at desks for two children with chalk and small slates and of course with pencils. I would think that it would be a year later that we progressed to a pen with a nib and ink in inkwells sunk into the desk. Biros had not been invented. We learnt our multiplication tables or 'times tables' as we called them – by chanting them together with the teacher. I was keen to learn and so I often repeated the process alone in bed before going to sleep, that way we were told we would remember them (years later French verbs were memorised in the same way).

My first pair of plimsolls (trainers weren't invented yet) were a simple joy to me. They were so comfortable and light, I felt very agile in them. But they were only to be worn for PE and games. I remember the small running track in the playground and the heat of the tarmac through my plimsolls on a summer's day. The summers at that school always seemed long and hot. On Friday afternoons we were allowed to take a toy to school but that would perhaps be only for the first term or two. Most children lived in the vicinity of the school so they went home for lunch. But I did have one friend who came by bus or car from Papplewick Pumping Station (a distance of 10-12miles) - I learned recently that her family are still in the area.

At the end of my first term at Seely School I had an accident! It was exactly a week before Christmas and on a Wednesday. There had been a fall of snow and my brother and I had made a wonderful slide the length of the back garden. I came home from school at midday and played on the slide while waiting to be called for lunch. Alas! I reached the end of the slide and sat on my left arm, which I had put down on the ice twisted backwards. I heard it crack! It didn't hurt immediately so I didn't cry, but went in to tell my mother I had broken my arm. She went very pale, but went straight to fetch our neighbour Miss Lawrence who was a retired nurse. This kind lady rested my arm on a cushion and called the doctor. He came and said I must go to hospital and I must not have any dinner because I would need an anaesthetic. Then I cried because it was to have been my favourite pudding (apple snow!) Also, it was the afternoon of the school Christmas party.

My father returned from the office and took me to Nottingham General Hospital where we waited for four hours before I received attention. My arm was set under anaesthetic and put in a splint. My blouse and underwear had been pushed up my arm so that my mother had to cut them all off to undress me. She wasn't very pleased. I was taken to school ten minutes before the end of the Christmas party, but in time to receive a present from Father Christmas.

My father continued to grow vegetables though he no longer had an allotment. There was a patch of raspberry canes and each summer a row of tomato plants along a South facing fence. My brother and I were allotted a small piece of garden each in which we could grow what we liked. Harry grew tall plants like golden rod and Michaelmas daisies so that he could make a den. The first thing I remember growing was a colourful display of Virginia stock, but I soon progressed to lettuce, radish and spring onions. Before long I had my own small pair of shears to help my father trim the edges of the lawn. A few years later I became adept at trimming hedges and thereafter became the family's chief hedge cutter – there being five stretches of privet hedge to keep tidy. As I grew up into my teens the neighbours often commented that I ought to be out with a young man instead of cutting hedges. But I loved gardening of any kind.

While we were young it was quite safe to play in the road as there was very little traffic. In winter we snowballed and made slides on the road. In summer we played hopscotch and rode our bikes on the pavement. We made use of a high wall opposite for cricket and tennis. We would stop to let the occasional car pass by. Of our near neighbours I can only remember two who had cars. The gentleman next door had a highly polished Wolsey and my friend Madge's father a somewhat smaller Ford 10 he called Bunty. Mr Perkins teased me for many years about the day I first knocked on his door and asked, "Can Madge come out to play?" He apparently said "What's your name?" and I replied "Eleanor Mary Green and I live at number 26." "Well, you had better come in," he said. From that day to this Madge and I have been friends and we have never fallen out. In many ways we have been as different as chalk from cheese but have always got along famously. As Madge was an only child her parents treated me as a second daughter and I loved them dearly.

On Sunday afternoons in the summer, they would take me with them for a drive into the countryside, perhaps into Derbyshire or Charnwood Forest even as far as Northamptonshire or a favourite spot in the Vale of Belvoir where we had tea in a garden at Knipton where the stream was crossed by a wooden plank. But more often than not it would be to Sherwood Forest or The Dukeries as it was usually called in those days. Here we would explore the Birch woods or visit the Major Oak and always in the late summer pick blackberries. We would hear the cuckoo and listen for woodpeckers and I loved to hear the sigh of the wind in the trees. To me this was paradise – a town girl being treated to a taste of the countryside and I loved every minute of it. I would go as often as they would invite me. I can hear Madge's mother saying, "Mind the ditch, Frank," or "Look there's a lovely log. Do stop and pick it up." They knew Derbyshire so well that she would sometimes say, "There's a lane we've not been down," and her dutiful husband would turn the car in order to explore a little bit more of their favourite countryside.

My parents didn't own a car but they did take us into the countryside occasionally. They had some friends Mr & Mrs Starkey, who seemed to me to be very elderly, who lived at Edwalton when it was just a small village. We usually went on Saturday afternoons in summer sitting upstairs on the number 25 bus from Nottingham. It took us what we called the 'long way round' picking us up in Sherwood and passing through Woodthorpe, up over Mapperley Plains and down through Gedling before setting out via West Bridgford to Edwalton. We had to alight before the village and walk the last lap past some very large houses with stripey lawns which always fascinated me.

The Starkeys lived at the far end of the village in a very old thatched cottage next to the church. Mr Starkey was a keen gardener and had a very large garden in three sections. In front of the cottage was an immaculate lawn where we played clock golf. At the side, near the entrance was always a bank

11

of bedding plants forming a word like 'Victory' or 'Peace' or a floral pattern with a wide weed-free gravel drive leading to the front door. Behind the house was another lawn where they could sit quietly without being overlooked. On the end of a large outbuilding was a huge water butt where my naughty brother Harry would deliberately leave the tap running. But the largest section of the garden ran from the side of the cottage to the Churchyard boundary. A central beautifully manicured grass path about six feet wide led to a lych gate into the churchyard. To the right of this path were vegetables, currant bushes, raspberries, sweet peas, hollyhocks and numerous herbaceous plants. To the left were apple, pear and plum trees in great variety and beneath them, in spring, daffodils and tulips and in early summer there would be forget-me-nots, primroses and polyanthus in their masses. On the far left was a narrow path just wide enough to walk beside the boundary hedge, beneath which were masses of deep purple violets. I have never seen so many violets under one hedgerow anywhere else ever!

This section of the garden was a great joy to me. I am certain now that this is the place that made a tremendous impression on me, and from that experience evolved a budding gardener and a wish to grow fruit and vegetables to eat and to grow plants and flowers in abundance in order to emulate Mr Starkey's cottage garden.

During the afternoon Harry and I would be sent to a farm in Edwalton village with a tin can to fetch the milk for tea and I remember passing the garden of the village postman, who boasted that no weed could be found on his patch. I believe he was right for all I ever saw there was a blaze of colour.

Sometimes we would go and play in the field beyond the Church where daisies and buttercups grew. Here I first saw oak apples in the hedgerow. There were usually cows in the field but they were friendly and I would sit in the grass making daisy chains. It was here that I announced to my father at a very early age that I was going to marry a farmer – and I did!

At tea time we had a wonderful spread. There was usually cold chicken or ham with salad, piles of homemade bread and butter, homemade cakes, and scones with cream and strawberries from the garden. But my mother always warned us, "Look carefully," as dear old Mrs Starkey was partially blind and didn't always notice the mould on the bread! I didn't let that worry me – I always enjoyed my tea at Edwalton.

When, at the end of a perfect afternoon, it was time to leave, Mr and Mrs Starkey would get out the bus timetable to see what time we could get a Barton's bus from the end of the village. This was the country bus that would take us to Nottingham Bus Station where we would then catch a local bus home. We would have our hands full as we were always laden with produce from their garden. There would be fruit and vegetables – I remember the most enormous leeks – and cut flowers too. We visited this elderly couple in their delightful cottage and garden for many years and I was very sad when they eventually died. Sadly too, the garden has now been built on but the cottage remains, though it has been modernised. The memories of that most delightful spot will remain with me forever.

My mother took us to church regularly but my father wouldn't go. He said it reminded him too much of the First War. We attended St. Martin's Church in Sherwood and I remember the church being built in 1937. It had been preceded by a small building on the Sherwood Estate fondly referred to as the 'Tin Tabernacle'. Our first vicar was Reverend Edward Lysons. We were all very proud of our new church and I made many friends there during later years when we had young people's services. Some of my early boyfriends sang in the choir, served at the altar or carried the Crucifix – the supreme honour – it was fairly high church.

Our vicar would not allow fundraising events, but sat outside the church one day each year when parishioners could go and donate gifts of money. There were always large congregations and one of my duties was to count people coming in for the 9am communion so that we knew how much bread and wine would be required. There were regularly about 90 – 100 people! One family came from the other side of Nottingham in a Lagonda car and when the sons grew up and began to drive, they occasionally came on their own. Then they would give me a lift home standing on the running board! I don't think there was a law against such practice in those days.

Chapter 3

THE WAR YEARS

It was 1939 and I was ten years old. We had just returned from our two-week summer holiday at Hoylake, on the Wirral peninsular in Cheshire. For some time there had been an air of expectancy that we might soon be plunged into war but, for us, we had enjoyed the lovely sandy beach and the warm sea, swam in the huge open-air swimming pool and followed my father round the golf course. We had skipped through the hot dusty streets singing the latest songs – 'Little Sir Echo' and 'South of the Border, Down Mexico Way'.

Little did we think that within two years my brother Harry would be old enough to join the armed forces. It probably crossed our parents' minds and no doubt worried them, but I had no thoughts in that direction at that time. Now, back home, the news on the wireless became serious. At the beginning of September Hitler invaded Poland, one of our allies, and Britain had no option but to support them and declare war on Germany. So, on Sunday 3rd September we all sat with our ears 'glued' to the wireless to hear the Prime Minister – Neville Chamberlain – state that Britain was "Now at war with Germany." I had no idea what this meant and how it would affect us, but to a ten-year-old girl it was quite frightening.

There was talk of air-raids and air-raid warnings, bombings, of possible gas attacks, food rationing and shortages of all kinds of things. We were not able to return to school on the appointed day due to preparations for war, but we went in small numbers (perhaps three or four classes at a time) for half a day, or to another local venue such as a church hall or a chapel room, for certain lessons. I well remember going to a nearby chapel room for history lessons which were taken by a Canadian teacher named Miss Muirhead. Every morning before the lesson began, she had us all singing 'We're Gonna Hang Out the Washing on the Siegfried Line'. This was a favourite morale booster at the time as it meant our soldiers would reach the German line and defeat them.

When air-raid shelters had been built in the school grounds we were allowed back to school full-time. However, the shelters had been built of brick above ground and were cold and damp and we never felt safe in them. Luckily there were few occasions when we needed to use them.

Winter approached and rationing of food began in earnest. I cannot remember which foods were rationed and when but, eventually, things like margarine (as there was very little butter), sugar, tea, coffee, sweets and chocolates, meat and cheese were all rationed. We never saw oranges, lemons or bananas throughout the whole of the war, as these could not be imported as the ships were all needed to carry troops or ammunition. Bread was not rationed until after the war. Later in the war a neighbour's son brought home some lemons and he gave me one. I took it to school and cut it up among my friends to eat.

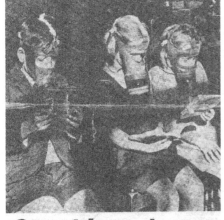

Countdown to war

;ASMASKS were issued to all British citizens on August 28, 1939

Everyone was fitted with a gas mask as it was feared gas would be used against us as it was in the First War. These were horrible things to wear, but we were compelled to practice wearing them for about twenty minutes every day at school until we got used to them. They absolutely terrified some children. We carried them <u>everywhere</u> in a square cardboard box slung over our shoulder. Babies who were too small to wear a

16

conventional gas mask were put in a kind of incubator. As the war progressed it became evident that no gas would be used against us and we ceased to carry these horrible masks.

We had snow before Christmas that year, and all through January and February of 1940 it was extremely heavy.

In those days it was quite usual to have lots of snow in these months and we always kept a spade or large shovel in the house. We often had to dig ourselves out in the morning. It was an occasion for Harry and I to get up earlier than usual to dig a channel along the front path (about 35 feet) before we went to school. Often there would be a foot of snow and we would pile it up at the side of the path. When we came home from school, we would then clear a path along the pavement in front of our house. All residents were expected to do this, but many didn't.

Of course, we had snowball fights and built snowmen, but our favourite pastime was sliding. Our best and longest slide we made on the road outside our house as there was very little traffic even in good weather. During the war there was even less traffic as petrol was strictly rationed and unobtainable for pleasure.

The winter of 1940 was most memorable as we had much more, and deeper, snow than any other year in my lifetime. On Perry Road we walked along the pavements level with the tops of the hedges (around 5 feet), where the snow had drifted in the wind. On the road it would be up to our knees and we would often have 'wellies' full of snow! Because houses then didn't have central heating the snow stayed on the roofs for days on end, several inches of it. Then, on a sunny day, it would start to thaw and drip. By teatime it would freeze again and the drips turned to icicles. They would hang from the eaves and guttering several inches, or sometimes feet, long. It had been known for falling icicles to kill people. When eventually we had a night without frost, the snow would slip of the roofs – whole masses of it at once. It was incredible! Many times, I was awoken by this frightening noise which sounded just like thunder. The frost used to make some lovely patterns on the INSIDE of the windows.

We spent a lot of time queuing during the war. We queued for everything. We queued for all kinds of food, especially if there had been a delivery after a shortage and word got around that a certain shop had some butter, or something which was very scarce. We queued for buses everywhere. There were fewer buses, as many of the drivers and conductors were required to join the armed forces and there would of course be a shortage of petrol for the buses (a conductor stood on the platform at the back of the bus, where he rang the bell for you to get off). My Dad became a volunteer conductor.

There were also the 'clippies', women who would walk through the bus checking bus passes and issuing tickets which they punched in a small machine hung around their neck and in front of them. Buses would be packed to capacity with perhaps a dozen people also standing in the gangway. Often, they would stop to pick up and cram two or three people on, then say, "Sorry! We are full up." We then had to wait for the next bus. Sometimes four or five would drive right by before one stopped.
I remember one Easter Saturday we waited for ages to go into town and couldn't get on, so we crossed the road and went the other way back to the terminus.

We queued for the cinema (we called it 'the Pictures'), sometimes for several hundred yards. You never saw a cinema without a queue.

Dancing at the Mikado.
My friend Madge and I joined a ballroom dancing class which was held above the Mikado Café on Long Row in Nottingham. (It is now part of the Debenhams store.) We were taught by Nancy Clarke who, many years later (in the 1970's), I saw on TV judging the original Come Dancing programme. She must have been a good teacher!

To get to the class we had to go by bus and walk a bit at both ends of the journey. One week Madge's mum would take us and the next week my mum would take us. The 'blackout' meant there were no street lights and it was extremely dark. We would hang on to either side of Mum and, holding a torch, as we got to every pavement curb we would say "Up," or "Down." That is how dark it was!

As the class was held above a café and cake shop there was always a wonderful aroma of coffee and baking – I can smell it now!

Nottingham was lucky as it wasn't bombed as frequently as some cities, although there were a few very bad air-raids, mostly at night. The nearest to us was a stick of five bombs, one of which fell at the end of our road. One person was killed and my father found a night- watchman at a small factory trembling uncontrollably in a traumatic state. He brought him home and gave him a cup of strong tea laced with whisky. Then he took him home in daylight.

On another occasion just one bomb fell in the Nottingham area (probably unloaded on the way back from Sheffield), in the garden of my brother's school-friend Keith. It made an enormous crater and moved the whole house one inch on its foundations. Next day the local press reported that Keith could be heard trying out the piano. The house had to be pulled down eventually.

MORNING AFTER: A scene in Nottingham after the raid

Many, many nights during 1941 and 1942 we went down to our Anderson shelter in the back garden. This was constructed of corrugated iron sheets and set about four feet into the ground. It was then covered with the soil that had been dug out and we planted it with rockery plants. Neighbours helped each other to erect these shelters. My father then built a wall of sand bags round the entrance where there was a short ladder. We had bunk beds, blankets and pillows and even an oil lamp, but we were still cold and damp. The reason for their frequent use was that German bombers raiding Sheffield (which they often did because of the steelworks) flew directly over us. Their droning sound gave us a sick feeling.

There was an anti-aircraft battery on Mapperley Plains which meant a lot of shrapnel from these shells dropped over and around our area. Indeed, after such a raid, Harry and I could sometimes pick up a couple of buckets full of shrapnel the next morning, from the school yard which was at the bottom of our garden. One incident in which we considered ourselves very lucky was one night when the order of our running to the shelter was changed. As I jumped the two shallow steps onto the lawn, a large piece of shrapnel fell beside me. Had my mother gone before me as she usually did, it would have hit her as she always walked around the steps, not down them. These air-raids were all very frightening and we missed a lot of sleep and went to school very tired.

When the air-raid sirens sounded we always got dressed and went downstairs, and if we didn't go into the shelter I tried to sleep on the settee, but not very successfully. Harry joined the Army in 1942 when he was seventeen and we missed him terribly. My mother was visibly distressed by his absence and the news we heard on the wireless. Later, when he went to France after D-Day in June 1944, she worried still more and a few months later mother died. I was just fifteen. She had had asthma badly for many years, but we were convinced it was the worry about the war that finally took her.

I had just begun my School Certificate year and found it very hard with all the homework and having to do the housework, washing, ironing and cooking all the meals for my father and me.

Chapter 4

SCHOOL DURING THE WAR YEARS

Despite the fact that I had passed the Eleven Plus Exam, my parents thought it would be more sensible for me to go to the local Secondary School than for me to have to travel the three-mile journey to Grammar School. So it was, though very disappointed, that I attended the Haywood School in 1940 and 1941. I did well here and was top of the class. My science teacher took us on field trips, pond dipping and cutting nettles for the war effort. I thoroughly enjoyed this. My music teacher, sorry to find I wasn't worthy of her school choir, encouraged me to join a pipe band. These pipes were like recorders, but we made them ourselves from lengths of one inch diameter bamboo and then we decorated them. Miss Gregson tuned them for us and we practiced a lot. We went off to other schools in Nottingham to play in concerts and competitions. It was all good fun. In 1942 my headmistress suggested to my parents that, as we were no longer experiencing daylight air-raids, they might consider me taking the Thirteen Plus Exam to get me into Grammar School. This I did and passed. I went into the third form at Manning Grammar School. What a joy!

Here I met Barbara and we formed a wonderful friendship which is still going strong after eighty plus years. At Manning we played hockey and tennis, we had a fully equipped gym and learned to swim at the local baths. Schoolwork was much harder and we had lots of homework, but I still managed to keep at or near the top of the class. I joined the School Guides but was not allowed to camp – only to visit with my mother. This really grieved me. She was rather overprotective, having lost one little girl.

In the summer term our history mistress Miss Pedley, who everyone adored, organised coach loads of us to help out at farms. This to me was wonderful. We went beet singling at Papplewick and Clifton, thistle pulling also at Clifton, potato picking at Bingham and pea picking on my uncle's farm at Tythby Grange. We also went flax pulling at Wollaton Park where the American GIs were camped. They would throw oranges over the high wire fencing to us. When D-Day arrived, they were gone.

On the way there and back in the coach, we sang our hearts out with all the 'Yankie' songs that were the hits at the time. In winter dinner breaks, these tunes boomed out again as we danced away in the school assembly hall. Once a week I spent my lunch break with a group of girls and a French lady - Madame Bongard - where we were only allowed to speak French. This helped me towards an 'A' later. A few of us were so keen on hockey that we regularly stayed after school and played for an hour with perhaps only four or five a side.

There was an incident in the fourth form in which I was involved. During the war fireworks were unobtainable, but a newsagent near home was selling 'Bengal lights' (long coloured matches). My friend Betty and I took orders from our form mates, and arrived early at school one morning with a satchel full each to sell. Having completed the transaction, one girl, Olive (who was a regular mischief maker), decided to surprise pupils in the next classroom. Barbara accompanied Olive as she struck and aimed a match into the centre of a group of girls. Unfortunately, a Mistress saw it happen and reported to the Head. Of course Betty and I were hauled out as well, and the four of us were sent home, each with a prefect and a letter to our parents – suspending us for a week! My mother was very cross with me so, when Dad was due home for lunch, I hid in the toilet. I was relieved to hear him say, "Good gracious! Is that all the child has done?" so I emerged.

This was a Friday and we had to go with a parent for an interview with the Head the following Tuesday. We each had a good telling-off and had to promise not to sell or lend anything in school again. We returned to school the next day but the episode was recorded in the minutes of the school. In the summer of 1943 Barbara's parents invited me to join their family on holiday in Derbyshire. Use of their car was confined to business, so we went by train to Chesterfield and then by bus to the small hamlet of Kelstedge, where we stayed on a farm.

Although food was rationed, there was an abundance of fresh produce like milk, eggs, chicken, home-made bread and fruit and vegetables from the garden. We added to these with cranberries and bilberries which we picked on the moors nearby. The farmer's wife made pies with these and skimmed cream from the milk – what a treat!

Having no wheels, we walked for miles in some beautiful countryside down narrow lanes and over the moors to Matlock. Behind the farm a rough footpath through the trees led down to a small wooden bridge over the stream. It was a picturesque spot known locally as 'The Trossachs'. Here we played for hours, carving little boats with our penknives and racing them on the water. We walked to the nearby village of Ashover to Church and to watch a cricket match, and I remember sliding down a steep muddy slope among the trees.

The farmhouse had no electricity, a gas mantle lit the living/dining room and we took candles up to bed. There was a washstand in the bedroom and a large jug of hot water outside our door in the morning. It was a most enjoyable two weeks and the only holiday I had during the war.

It was May 1945 and the end of the war was expected soon. Also approaching rapidly were our School Certificate Exams. First off was the French oral exam, when each girl went alone to the library to converse in French with Miss Potter, our French Mistress. After an enjoyable session I emerged from the library to be met by my friend Betty, who announced, "It's over." Eleven am had come and gone and the end of the war had been declared. We had beaten old Hitler – Peace at last! What a lot of rejoicing there was. No more exams were scheduled for that day and we were free to go home and celebrate.

After dashing home for a spot of lunch we went down into Nottingham city centre to join the revelry. There was dancing and singing and cheering as we stood for a while on Queen Street, overlooking a packed Market Square, taking it all in. Later as dusk fell, every conceivable kind of light was switched on until the whole city seemed ablaze. How wonderful it was after six years of darkness.

In the evening we went to the Arboretum, where a wooden floor had been laid near the bandstand for dancing. Here we danced the night away till we could dance no longer.

During the summer holidays that year there was a school harvest camp at Glenfield in Leicestershire. We didn't actually camp, but slept in the small village school – Glenfield was a tiny village in those days. We had taken our bikes as we were to cycle out to various farms to help with the harvest. There were no combine harvesters then. Corn was cut with a binder and we stooked the sheaves by hand. We enjoyed the work, but as it was hot our bare arms were scratched to bits by the straw. We had to buy cream from the village shop to sooth them. Some days we worked in a park where we had to lift our bikes over gates - most were heavy, solid, war-time bikes. One day it rained so we had a day off. We persuaded the school caretaker to make up the fire in the boiler room below and found a long tin bath. Three or four of us took a turn at sitting in it in front of the blazing fire. After drying and dressing, we got on our bikes and cycled into Leicester to the pictures and promptly fell asleep!

We were at Glenfield for two weeks and while there the war ended in the Far East and VJ day was announced. This called for more celebrations. Luckily we had a cookery mistress with us and she (Miss Pye) baked an enormous cake.

The staff dressed up in exquisite home-made costumes and we were allowed to spend the evening dancing in the local pub yard.

When I returned to school in September 1945, having gained satisfactory results in the School Certificate, I entered the sixth form (commercial) and made a new friend - Margaret. Here we concentrated on shorthand, typing, book-keeping, and commercial English.

My father did not wish me to pursue a career in horticulture as I had wanted, but thought a job in a bank or office would be more suitable for a young lady. The course was enjoyable enough and I passed my RSA exams at the end of it, but did not relish the thought of being stuck in an office for evermore.

In April 1946 Margaret's parents invited me to join their family for a day in London. I jumped at the idea as I had never visited the capital. We went by train (steam, of course) and I remember vividly the devastation from the German bombing on the outskirts of the city. Large areas of suburban housing were so badly damaged they were uninhabitable. Other areas were totally wiped out. We had seen pictures in the newspapers and heard reports on the wireless but of course there was no television, so it was difficult to imagine the reality of the destruction. It was heart-breaking to see and made us realise how lucky we had been in Nottingham.

The purpose of our visit was mainly to see the lilac in bloom at Kew Gardens and it didn't disappoint. It was truly magnificent which lifted our spirits. We had time for some sightseeing in Central London but everywhere there were piles of rubble and large empty spaces with just 'nothing'. Our visit was a history lesson not to be missed but we were happiest among the lilac trees in 'nature's wonderland'.

Go down to Kew in lilac time,
It isn't far from London,
And you shall wander hand in hand,
In love with nature's wonderland,
Go down to Kew in lilac time,
It isn't far from London.

Before I began work in September, there was another exciting holiday to be had. Margaret belonged to a Baptist Church at New Basford in Nottingham and I had been along and met some of her friends there on several Sundays. Among them was a lady doctor from Bulwell, who was organising a visit to the Keswick Convention in the Lake District. To make it attractive to teenagers they were intending to camp and have a programme of recreational activities including mountaineering, rowing, tennis etc. They invited me to join them. This sounded too good to miss, especially as I'd never been to the Lake District. The only problem was that Margaret and I had a typing exam on the Monday after they proposed to set off. Once the exam had been taken, we could then leave school. This was July 1946.

So it was that the rest of the Baptist Church party left Nottingham on the Saturday and set up camp just outside Keswick at Portinscale. Apparently, it was so hot that milk, butter etc. had to be kept in the nearby stream. But on the Monday, it began to rain and the ground became so waterlogged that they had to abandon the campsite. When Margaret and I arrived by train on the Tuesday, we found they had moved everything into the Drill Hall in Keswick and there we stayed for the rest of the two weeks, sleeping on paillasses (straw mattresses) on the Hall floor.

Derwentwater.
It rained most mornings, but we went off to one of the religious meetings at the Convention which was held in a large marquee in the park. Most

afternoons were free and we played tennis or rowed on Derwentwater or ventured up one of the local mountains. The evenings were often glorious after the rain and my vivid memory is of climbing Cat Bells on a lovely sunny evening and seeing the view over Derwentwater towards the Skiddaw range of mountains. It was a wonderful holiday and I met some very friendly people. The Lake District has remained a favourite holiday spot ever since.

Chapter 5

STARTING WORK (1946-1947)

Back home, my first job was waiting for me at the beginning of September. I joined the War Agricultural Executive Committee (known nationwide as the 'War Ag') as a shorthand typist. This was about as near as I could get to farming and horticulture in an office. The War Ag had been set up by the Government at the beginning of the war to help farmers plan the crops they must grow, because very little food could be imported. Ships were required to carry troops and ammunition not foodstuffs. Pasture had to be ploughed up to grow food crops and even people like us dug up our lawns to grow vegetables as part of the Dig for Victory campaign.

After the war the War Ag carried on for some years until Britain was back on its feet again.

So here I was in their office at Weekday Cross in Nottingham, taking shorthand from the bosses of various departments and bashing away at a typewriter. All the staff were very friendly and I made many friends, the main ones being Audrey, Joyce and Eileen. Eileen eventually married the top Executive Officer and came to live at Thurgarton where I visited her occasionally. Joyce's parents lived at Eastwood and had a caravan at Watnall where I visited at weekends on several occasions. Audrey became a very good friend and introduced me to youth hostelling.

Our first adventure together was in January 1947 to Ilam Hall in Derbyshire. We went by train or bus (probably both) to Ashbourne on the Friday evening, and walked up the steep hill and out through Fenny Bentley the six miles to Ilam with a big rucksack each on our backs and snow underfoot. We cooked food in the communal kitchen and I remember asking two lads what it was that they were cooking, "Climbing food," came the reply – it looked a bit nondescript.

We stayed two nights and went walking in the Manifold Valley in daytime. There were to be many more of these youth hostel weekends with Audrey – mostly in Derbyshire and on foot, but some on bikes elsewhere.
Now began more than two months of ice and snow which broke all records. It snowed almost every day until, by the end of the month, 38 inches (965mm) had fallen and there were 8-foot snow drifts in our area. When we had dug ourselves out of our houses, we walked along the pavements level with the top of the hedge as we had done in 1940.

On February 19th, the 32nd night of continuous frost was recorded and we had frequent power cuts. In those days there was no central heating at all, we just had a coal fire in the living room and a gas cooker in the kitchen. Our houses were pretty cold anyway and we were obliged to wear more clothes - woollen ones. Girls all wore liberty bodices as well as a vest. They never wore trousers, only skirts. It was a long time before girls wore trousers and even longer before adult women did.

Power cuts meant no electricity for lighting, so we spent hours sitting huddled together round the fire, with candles. Hot water bottles accompanied us to bed, but in the morning, there were lovely patterns on the inside of the window that Jack Frost had left during the night.

Then suddenly on March 8th the big freeze broke, when the temperature soared to 42°F or 5.5°C and then we had the heaviest rainfall for 58 years – 13 inches (330mm) in a 24-hour period. This of course brought widespread and very serious flooding. At the time I was secretary to the County Land

Drainage Officer and our department became extremely busy. We had to hire land drainage equipment from counties as far away as Devon and Cornwall.

When the flood waters had receded, my boss took me to see the devastation at Gringley Carr in the north of Nottinghamshire, where thousands of acres of farmland had been under water for several weeks and entire crops were ruined. Large trees bore marks showing the height of the flood water, which must have been 20 feet in places.

When things were back to normal I was due for a week's holiday and I went alone by train to visit my Aunt and Uncle in Taunton. I arrived to find a foot of snow there and I had to trudge through it to their house, in the dark.

Back at the office we had a good social life, lots of parties and dances and in the summer, numerous outings. There were camps for E.V.W.s (European Volunteer Workers) at Langar and at Nether Headon (Nr. Retford). One of the departments organised these people to work on local farms and they invited us to their camps for dances.

Another but quite different type of work camps were V.A.C.s (Volunteer Agricultural Camps) where anyone could go to help with farm work, usually at harvest time, as part of the war effort. These still operated until the end of the 1940s. Those of us working for the War Ag could get a second week at one of these camps if we took a week of our own allotted holiday there. Audrey and I did this on several occasions – at Henley-on-Thames and Windsor in October 1947 and Forest Hill near Oxford in 1948. We also went to one at Kenilworth in Warwickshire in May 1949.

Volunteering with harvest at Oxford Agricultural Camp 1948

Each time we went by train and took our bikes, cycling out to the farms every day. Two things I remember about Kenilworth – we met a chap with long hair (very rare in those days as it was the era of 'short back and sides') and very fine features. He said he was a life model for the sculptor, Sir Jacob Epstein. The second was a day at Warwick cemetery clipping around the grave stones.

It had been raining and there was no work on the farms for Thursday and Friday. We were nearly out of money and told the Camp Warden we would have to go home early if he couldn't find us work for the next two days. It was an easy job but we were a bit upset when we came to a disturbed grave and were told by cemetery workers there had been an exhumation the previous night.

Because there had been a shortage of work, we had been able to use our bikes to visit Stratford-on-Avon, Warwick and Leamington Spa.

My brother Harry spent some time in India with the Army after the war had ended and when he returned home in the summer of 1947, Dad and I went to Liverpool to see the ship dock (The Empress of Canada). There were so many troops on board that when they all came to one side of the ship to wave to us, the ship began to list and an announcement was made for them to disperse. As soon as Harry was de-mobbed from the Army we all three had a holiday at Bridlington. Here we met a family of four sisters from Gargrave in Yorkshire. One of the sisters was in a wheelchair, but the other three were keen horse-riders and persuaded Harry and I to go with them to a local riding centre and have a go on a horse. Luckily, I had a pair of trousers (slacks they were called in those days) and we bought crepe bandages for our legs to stop chafing. I enjoyed the ride across the fields and along the beach tremendously, but Harry was a bit scared and had wrapped the reins round and round his fingers which were a bit raw by the end of the morning. Another day we went flying in a small aircraft over Bridlington Bay which was a first for us both. Afterwards we played bowls on the green opposite the hotel which was new to all three of us.

Visit to Cromford.
Also that summer, my father and I took Madge with us for a week in Derbyshire. We stayed in a house near Cromford and were very well looked after by a lady who lived there alone. She had a big garden full of vegetables and some chickens, further along the road she owned a field where she kept a cow. In the early morning we saw her walk there with her bucket and

having milked the cow by hand, returned with fresh milk for our breakfast. There were also eggs aplenty and lots of home-made bread. In the evening we had salad from the garden with cold chicken or ham.

When out walking one evening along the road towards Whatstandwell we came to a tree-covered area and there, crossing the road, were hundreds of baby frogs. They were coming from a rock-covered hill on our right, on their way to a steep grass field which ran down to the river. We were able to pick them up and play with them, which gave us an idea. The following evening, we returned with a match-box each in order to capture one. How they survived overnight I'm not sure, but they did. The next day it rained so we went to the pictures in Matlock and whilst there we released the frogs. It's not only teenage boys who are bad – girls can be just as cruel without realising it.

Chapter 6

YOUTH HOSTELLING (1948-1949)

At Easter 1948 Barbara and I made the first of many cycle trips to Houghton Mill in Huntingdonshire. This became one of our favourite youth hostels as we could cycle down the old A1 with very little traffic. We could visit places like Ely and St. Ives (not the Cornish one) when we had a Bank Holiday Monday tagged onto the weekend.

That May we did our first long cycle run to Taunton in Somerset to visit my Aunty Bill and Uncle Laurie. On the Saturday we cycled from home in Nottingham to Stratford-on-Avon Youth Hostel and in the evening went to the Shakespeare Memorial theatre.

The next day we cycled through the Vale of Evesham to Cleeve Hill near Cheltenham. The youth hostel here was a hut with an old tin roof, set on the hillside. When it was fine you could clearly see the Welsh mountains. That night it poured with rain, hammering on the old tin roof. Next morning, we found crumbs all over the floor. During the night a mouse had located and eaten Barbara's biscuits.

Our next youth hostel was at Batheaston, near Bath. The following morning soon after Bath, the first fox I had ever seen crossed the road in front of us and disappeared into some woods. On we cycled down through Cheddar Gorge where we visited Wookey Hole. That night at Croscombe Youth Hostel, there was a party of school children - probably 9 or 10 years old - and we

34

were impressed with how organised they were when passing up their plates, cutlery etc. after the meal.

Barbara & I in Cheddar Gorge May 1948

The following day we paid a visit to the beautiful cathedral at Wells and also to Glastonbury Abbey. We were due to arrive in Taunton the following day, but we had a hard slog in a gale which was trying to push us into the ditch. We really didn't know whether to laugh or cry. Eventually a small lorry stopped and offered us a lift for the last 19 miles into Taunton. What a relief!

We spent a lovely week with Auntie and Uncle, visiting various places of interest with them and we returned home by train with our bikes in the guard's van.

The following year (1949) I became friendly with Joan Armitage who worked in the milk department at the War Ag, going out in the early morning to take milk samples from farms before it was collected. She belonged to a canoe club which had its HQ at Bloors Café near Trent Lock and she invited me to join them. There was a big shed beside the café where they kept some very old wooden canoes (singles and doubles) and all their equipment. They had the use of a veranda where they could shelter from the elements and eat their own packed lunches.

During the summer we sometimes camped in the field at the back. We persuaded the British Canoe Union to hold the National Sprint Championships on the Trent instead of on the Thames at Teddington. So we built four wooden racing canoes ready for the event. My friend Joan won the ladies' race.

At the end of the month Nottingham held its Quincentenary celebrations and the Canoe Club was invited to give a demonstration at Trent Bridge in Nottingham. There was jousting and a greasy pole and then we raced in our new canoes. They were quite narrow and wobbly and as I got into mine, I capsized and got a soaking. There was a tremendous cheer from a crowd of 30,000 people!

Canoes we built for 1949 National Sprint Championship at Nottingham Quincentenary Celebrations

At the beginning of August my French pen-friend Huguette came to stay and we visited Newstead Abbey, Wollaton Hall, Haddon and Hardwick Halls in Derbyshire, and finished up with a few days sightseeing in London.

Later that month Barbara and I set off on our second cycling holiday. I had been told how pretty Oxfordshire was, so we went by train to Woodford near Banbury, staying the first night at Hanwell Castle Youth Hostel. We set off on our bikes through Bloxham with its handsome tall spire and visited the Rollright Stones near Chipping Norton. By the afternoon we had found Great Tew with its picturesque village green with ancient stocks and surrounded by huge elm trees. There was a row of pretty thatched cottages. We decided on a picnic tea on the green and set our stall out. As it was Barbara's birthday her mum had made us a cake. Barbara went to a cottage door with our 'billycan' to ask for some water to make our tea (we had a small stove with us). The lady said she would make the tea and call us when it was ready.

When Barbara went to collect it, she said, "Bring your friend," and we were surprised to find she had laid the table with a substantial afternoon tea for us. Only then did Barbara disclose that it was actually her birthday. What a lovely surprise.

Barbara's alfresco birthday tea 1949

That night we stayed at Charlbury Youth Hostel and I remember we argued as to who should have the top bunk. We had agreed on alternate nights, but as it was Barbara's birthday she must have thought she was entitled to it. I don't remember the outcome but I think it was the only time we ever had an argument. Next morning, we found Minster Lovell, an exceptionally pretty village with the river Windrush running beside a large cricket field. From there we went on to Woodstock where Barbara had a puncture, quickly repaired in the grounds of Blenheim Palace, the birthplace of Sir Winston Churchill. We arrived in Oxford in time to do some sightseeing but agreed we would stop there on the way back to see more.

It was at Oxford that we joined the Thames towpath and followed it all the way to London, but first to Henley-on-Thames via numerous picturesque villages and passing eleven river locks. We liked Henley and could have spent longer there but we had booked a night at the National Cyclists' Union (NCU) hostel at Shepperton Lock, so we moved on, as we would have a long gruelling ride into London the next day via Eton, Windsor and Runnymede.

Once in London we stayed the first night at Central London Youth Hostel in Great Ormond Street so that we were close to the Royal Albert Hall where, that evening, we saw the French cellist Pierre Fournier at a Promenade Concert. Barbara is very musical and played the cello herself at that time. The next day was devoted to more sightseeing and a visit to Hampton Court Palace. That night we moved to Highgate Youth Hostel and later went to the theatre.

YOUTH HOSTELS ASSOCIATION
(ENGLAND & WALES)
National Office: Welwyn Garden City, Herts.

1953

Y HA

I YHF

Member of the International
Youth Hostel Federation

DATE	GROUP	MEMB. No.	FEE REC'D
16 2 53	NM	196965	10°

MISS E. GREEN
26 PERRY ROAD
SHERWOOD
NOTTINGHAM.

Y. H. A. (ENGLAND AND WALES)
WELWYN GARDEN CITY

Profession Veterinary Surgeon . Date of Birth. 2-3-29

DECLARATION
(This card is not valid until signed in ink by the member)

I agree to abide by the rules and regulations of the Association
as printed in the current National Handbook and undertake not
to use any hostel if I have recently been in contact with any
infectious disease.

Signed .... Eleanor M. Green ....

OBJECTS OF THE ASSOCIATION
To help all, especially young people of limited
means, to a greater knowledge, love and care of
the countryside, particularly by providing hostels
or other simple accommodation for them in their
travels, and thus to promote their health, rest and
education.

It was time to turn north again and head for home. This time we cycled over
the Chiltern Hills which tested our stamina. It was a long ride through
Beaconsfield and High Wycombe, but eventually we found the youth hostel
at Speen. The next morning as we entered the small market town of Thame
the church bells were ringing and we agreed that we must go to church. As
we were wearing shorts and tops (the name T-shirt was years away) we felt a
little self-conscious, so we sat in the pews right at the back. After the service
the vicar's wife spotted us and said how nice it was to see us among the
congregation. We apologised for our scant clothing, but she insisted that it
didn't matter one bit what we wore as long as we went to church and
promptly invited us to the vicarage for coffee.

Soon after Thame we came across Waterperry House purely by chance. I was
delighted to find it as it was one of the only two Horticultural Colleges for
girls in the country and I would have loved to have been a student there.
Back in Oxford we had time for more sightseeing and stayed overnight again.
We spent the following morning in the 'City of Dreaming Spires' before

cycling back up the road to Hanwell for our last stopover, and then caught the train home to Nottingham the next day.

I did keep a record of mileages as I had a cyclometer on the front wheel of my bike, but they appear to have gone astray. I estimate this trip would have covered about 300 miles cycling.

My love of sport prompted me to join the school Old Girls' hockey team. This continued for about five years. In summer, as well as spending a lot of time watching matches at Trent Bridge, I played cricket for Nottingham Women's Casuals. There was one memorable match played on the Nottingham University ground where we were all struck by lightning! It had been thundering but not raining, so we carried on playing. Our team was fielding when suddenly an enormous thunderbolt knocked us all to the ground.

Luckily we all got up, but the hair of the girl nearest me stood straight up – she had two metal grips in it. My own hair crackled alarmingly, needless to say we all dashed to the pavilion and then the rain fell heavily.

Manning School Old Girls' Hockey team 1946/7

Nottingham Women's Casuals Cricket Team 1946/7

Chapter 7

MY VETERINARY JOB (1950)

Our plans for this year included a mammoth cycling tour of Scotland along with Barbara's brother Jack and his friend Geoff, with our ultimate aim to climb Ben Nevis. But first I had another exciting adventure to prepare for. I had been offered a job as a Veterinary Assistant with the Ministry of Agriculture – outdoors on farms all over the county dealing with cattle, pigs, sheep and poultry (no small domestic animals) and most importantly, no more bashing at a typewriter in a stuffy office!

My father wasn't too pleased despite the fact that his own father had been a vet. I was just 21 and now an adult and could choose my career and get my hands dirty if I wanted to! But first I had to learn to drive! No formal lessons were offered, but I was sent by my boss to an old aerodrome near Retford which was a Ministry of Agriculture Depot. The first day I had some basic instruction and then drove a selection of vans and trucks out to surrounding towns with a driver beside me, delivering tools and equipment most days. After less than a month I passed my driving test.

Part of my new job involved the eradication of TB in cattle, the setting up of AI centres and freeing flocks of breeding poultry (including turkeys) of Salmonella by blood testing and culling the reactors. Training was given at the Ministry's Veterinary Laboratory near Weybridge in Surrey. I stayed with an aunt at Ealing who took me shopping in Oxford Street and to the theatre several times.

Back home my job sent me all over Nottinghamshire and into neighbouring counties, especially when there were outbreaks of foot and mouth disease, fowl pest or swine fever. The most memorable spell of 'detached duty' was in January of 1954 high up on the Yorkshire Moors in deep snow, not knowing the area. I often had to leave my car on the main road and walk to the farms. For two weeks I stayed in a private house in Leeds. They were pretty awful 'digs'. I had a room on the top floor with two beds. The rain poured in a steady stream onto one of the beds so I chose the other. There were three students in the next room who seemed to stay up all night making coffee on a small table just outside my bedroom door. I had very little sleep. Eventually there was a vacant room at the YWCA, so I moved.

On another occasion while I was with one of the vets TB testing a herd of Friesians, we had a frightening incident. We had tested the cows and young stock and there was just the bull to test. As the stockman led him from his loose box he careered round the farmyard knocking the man to the ground. Luckily the farmer managed to restrain the bull and got him into the cattle crush. I had jumped to the top rail of the crush out of reach!

Another unusual occasion was a case of fowl pest where 300 laying hens had to be slaughtered. I helped the farmer and his wife to 'neck' them and the carcasses were incinerated. Then lads from a nearby Young Offender Institution were brought in to scrub down and disinfect the three large chicken sheds. The problem was that the only water was from a well in the farmyard, and the pump had to be primed nine times before it would produce any water. Then it was carried to the field in buckets. It meant either someone pumping non-stop or there was a lot of priming to do.

We had several cases of foot and mouth disease in the 1950s and some were very tricky to trace. I remember one where imported beef carcasses came wrapped in very fine soft netting called 'scrim'. Somebody had found this ideal for cleaning windows, washing cars etc. and recommended it to his farmer brother for washing cows' udders. The stockman had washed the scrim in the cowshed and then used his feeding shovel to unblock the drain – nowhere near the cows' udders! The whole herd had to be slaughtered along with a large flock of sheep in an adjacent field. These crises were devastating for farmers and some had their livelihoods completely destroyed.

When blood-testing poultry for salmonella we stood outside in all weathers. At one large farm a group of lads helped and on a very cold day they would deliberately let the hens escape so that they get warm by chasing them back to their pens. The most pleasant days were where the poultry huts were in orchards. There was some protection given by the trees and in autumn we could eat the fruit. Turkeys were not our favourite as they were tested in January after the Christmas stock had departed. We often stood on a hillside in deep snow for this job and had to take a small tube full of blood from each one, instead of just a spot. Tricky with frozen fingers!

I thoroughly enjoyed that first year in my new job and carried on doing it for another six years, out of doors in the fresh air every day come rain or shine. (1951)

The second year there was an added bonus when a young veterinary student from Glasgow University, named David, joined me for his summer vacation. He accompanied me to the farms for some work experience and we got on well. Before resuming his studies at Glasgow, he took me to the Festival of Britain in London which was a most interesting and enjoyable day out.

Chapter 8

SCOTLAND CYCLING TOUR (Summer 1950)

It was summer and we had been planning our August cycling trip to Scotland. This time Barbara and I took her brother Jack and his pal Geoff with us. They were both professional photographers – Geoff in a top-class studio in Nottingham, and Jack with Rolls-Royce at Derby where he photographed aircraft parts (he remained there all his working life).

We set off from Nottingham on Friday 28th July on the overnight train to Glasgow, with our bikes in the guard's van – it was a steam train of course, no diesels for about another ten years. The train was packed and we were excited so didn't sleep much.

We took a long, cobbled road out of Glasgow and eventually found a café in the smart town of Dumbarton on the Clyde estuary. We continued on country roads through Boxhill to Alexandria, arriving at Loch Lomond Youth Hostel in bright sunshine. It was a huge building resembling a castle, set in large grounds stretching down to the loch-side road. The hostel had been acquired five years previously through aid from America, and we were there to see the official opening ceremony that evening by the American Consul.

First though, Barbara and I were given the job of picking armfuls of flowers from a walled garden to bedeck the hall. (At youth hostels everyone had a job to do either on arrival or before leaving next morning). During the ceremony a plaque was unveiled, there were pipers, dancing by a small boy and girl, Scottish Country dancing and local songs. There was a party of Americans, some Frenchmen and another group of English people. Each group sang one of their national songs and displayed their flag. We felt very privileged to be there that evening and to take part in a most enjoyable celebration. Next morning, we followed the road along the side of Loch Lomond in pouring rain, stopping for coffee and biscuits at a rather smart hotel in Luss. This is a very pretty village of bungalows with colourful gardens. It was originally built for workmen quarrying for slate but is now a real beauty spot. We have visited it in recent years on several occasions. On we pressed through the hamlet of Tarbet and between two mountains, whose peaks were invisible for clouds, onward and upward to Arrochar for lunch. After lunch we cycled around the head of Loch Long and across the River Croe and into Ardgarton, where the youth hostel was tucked away in a pine forest. Here we met two young teachers (Margaret & Doreen) from Skegness and two teenage Scots lads from Blairgowrie (Pandy & Butch) with whom we spent the evening playing cards. They showed us a variety of games of Patience and how to play Whist. Then they taught us lots of Scottish pronunciations.

The following morning was hard work. We pedalled our way up the 'Rest and Be Thankful' Pass – a gradual slope for about two miles but with a wonderful view from the top looking down into Glen Croe. Half way up Geoff had hung onto a small lorry until the driver spotted him and in a very polite way said, "I thought I was pulling more than my load."

After a welcome drink from a spring at the very top of the pass, we were able to freewheel from the 'Cobbler' down through Glen Kinglas to the head of Loch Fyne and beside the Loch to Inverary for lunch and shopping. The shops were full of lovely tartan items but it was too early in our tour to start spending or carrying souvenirs. That afternoon we saw major tree-felling operations and later I got stuck in a bog while looking at unfamiliar wild flowers, and had to remove my shoes and socks. We had a picnic tea by the roadside at Cladich while they dried. There was a long, uphill, flint road to the next youth hostel in a remote situation, near to the small village of Dalmally with one shop. The hostel was small and cosy with a friendly warden. We met a family from Swansea with two little girls whom we had seen at Ardgarton.

Leaving Dalmally in Strath of Orchy we passed round the head of Loch Awe in sight of Kilchurn Castle. Beneath the towering Ben Cruachan we cycled through the Pass of Brande, stopping at the magnificent Falls of Cruachan to take photos. At this spot Geoff took a superb photo of sheep being driven through the pass by two shepherds. (Many years later I did an oil painting of this scene. It hangs on my bedroom wall and remains a favourite.) Several miles of undulating country brought us to Connel where we dined at a small hotel. From the toll bridge which crossed Loch Etive, we looked out towards the Firth of Lorne and were only 6 miles from Oban, our nearest coastal resort. After purchasing eggs at a farm, we passed alongside the railway whose line crossed Loch Crearan by viaduct. So we climbed up the embankment, and struggled with each bike up a cinder track in pouring rain to take us over to Crearan.

On through Appin past the end of Loch Laich, Portnacroish and in sight of Shune Island we at last halted for a well-deserved tea, which we ate midst the heather on a mountainside overlooking Loch Linnhe. It was cold and very dull with huge black clouds overhead. We drank milk at a small farm and then pressed on to Ballachulish with its famous ferry across Loch Leven. Passing through the tiny village of whitewashed cottages and slate quarries, we spotted the Pap of Glencoe towering over more cottages, one of which supplied more milk. It was then only an easy ride beside a babbling brook through the beautiful Glen to reach Glencoe Youth Hostel. We had cycled 54 Scottish miles that day.

In the morning we felt quite excited to be aiming for Glen Nevis, where we hoped to climb the Ben the following day. We returned to Ballachulish and crossed Loch Leven by ferry. The day's provisions were purchased at Onich, and we continued beside the Loch to Fort William where we ate a hearty meal and bought souvenirs. The ride through the Glen was beautiful, only the road and a narrow river separating the youth hostel from Ben Nevis. The day was hot so, as we had arrived early, we took our cameras and went to explore. We were told that most climbers of the mountain forded the river to save a three mile walk into Fort William and back the other side. We decided to have a practice ready for the next morning and it was icy cold!

A group of young Americans, two French girls and the family from Swansea were with us again that night. In the evening we walked along the Glen in the twilight.

The day of the 'great ascent' (Thursday 3rd August) dawned bright and warm and we were all very excited. Being short of provisions we were obliged to

send the boys into Fort William early. Meanwhile Barbara and I forded the river and set off up the footpath. Beyond the bracken and slippery slopes, Geoff and Jack joined us and we proceeded on rough stone paths.

About halfway up we caught up with the Americans and the two French girls, at a fast-flowing stream which crossed our path. We proceeded together as the path narrowed and crossed a mountain torrent near a broken wooden bridge. Here was the last sign of vegetation and from there upwards there was nothing but scree and boulders. We had brief

48

glimpses of mountain lochens and passed lots of cairns. It was hard going and very rough. We reached the summit at about 2pm – the ascent having taken 4 hours. Near the top we found snow in a crevasse, and were elated when suddenly the cairn marking the summit appeared. There were also the ruins of an old meteorological station. We ate a sandwich lunch and took lots of photos.

Dave, one of the American boys, was taking photos for the National Geographic magazine. The Americans and French left the summit before us so we were a little behind, but we soon caught up with Jinx who had set off alone and lost the path. From then the descent was difficult as it was mostly loose scree which gave way under our feet, so we slid on our bottom some of the way. Arriving back at the broken bridge we found that Jacqueline, one of the French girls, had sprained her ankle and had to be carried by the boys, taking turns. The lower slopes were very slippery and necessitated removing shoes and boots. We were glad we had to paddle across the river again. Back at the hostel we had the luxury of a shower and then a whopping meal. We had been 5 hours coming down. I think we all slept well that night! The hostel warden did say we had been very lucky to have such a clear day, as nine days out of ten he couldn't see the summit.

Feeling very stiff and as if our legs didn't belong to us, we decided on an easy day. We shopped for souvenirs in Fort William and had lunch, before returning to Ballachulish via a different route. We arrived at Glencoe Youth Hostel in time for another meal and then walked to a nearby farm for more milk. We saw gypsies sitting round a fire on the way. Back at the hostel we met Mr and Mrs Brown and Hamish from Dollar in Clackmananshire and spent the evening talking to them and eating chocolate. They told us of their experiences in South Africa where Hamish was born, and Hamish recounted his many long cycling trips through Scotland.

On leaving Glencoe village the next morning, we began to climb the steep hill through Glencoe Pass and slowly cycled past the site of the massacre in 1692. A fine drizzle increased to a steady downpour as the day wore on.

After a brief drop on a winding road, we crossed the bleak Rannoch Moor in driving rain and a strong headwind. Geoff and Jack had gone on ahead and it was hard work – we weren't sure whether we wanted to laugh or cry! In the middle of all this we randomly came across a lone piper playing Scottish music by the roadside – he was absolutely drenched! Because of the weather we were unable to appreciate the beauty of the vast expanse of moorland, nor the lunch we ate at a café near Bridge of Orchy. A steady, rather long rise necessitated walking part of the way to Tyndrum, from where the road was easy to Crianlarich Youth Hostel on the River Dochart in Strath Fillan. It had been a tough ride but it was only the second time that we had had to don waterproofs.

Next morning we followed the River Dochart through the Glen and had coffee at the Luib Hotel. We by-passed Killin, but saw the spectacular Dochart Falls, then on through Glen Ogle to Lochearnhead for lunch. We took the road through Balquidder along the edge of Loch Voil to a small youth hostel up on a hill through a farmyard full of sheep, picking wild raspberries on the way. We had also visited Rob Roy's grave and the church at Balquidder. That evening we met Mike and Ken from Sandiacre and had a long chat with them.

As we had another day at Monachyle, Barbara and I decided to walk the 4 miles back to Kingshouse on the main road and get a bus to Strathyre where there were some nice shops. On arriving back at Kingshouse we got a lift with a farmer back to Monachyle Youth Hostel and then cycled two miles to fetch milk. That evening we walked up the hill behind the hostel where we had a wonderful view over Loch Voil and Loch Doine. It was a lovely spot, quite isolated and very peaceful.

Back at Strathyre, this time on our bikes, we stopped for coffee and biscuits and visited the Leny Falls before stopping in Callander for lunch and more shopping. We took the road into the Trossachs past Loch Vennachar. The Creag Dhu Youth Hostel was situated near Brig O' Turk in sight of Loch Achray. Mike and Ken from Sandiacre were there too. Later the warden made a big log fire and we all sat round for a sing-song led by the warden and Mike till 11:30pm.

The next day Mike and Ken had to return home due to shortage of cash. After meeting Mike, we kept in touch and he became a boyfriend of mine for about two years. He was a metallurgist at Raleigh and was one of the first to move out to India when they opened a factory there. He was a nice lad, but when you are 21 what's the good of a boyfriend in India?

Wednesday 9th August and we had planned to have a boat trip on Loch Katrine but it was pouring with rain, so we cycled to the expensive Pierhead Cafe for our usual mid-morning treat, and then ate our sandwich lunch huddled together under a canopy. No let-up in the weather, so cycled back to the pretty village of Creag Dhu in full view of Ben Ledi, Ben Venue and Ben An when fine. Later Ian Morrison and Colwyn Hunter introduced themselves, a Scot and a Welshman. After chatting for some time, we joined them for a walk. When we returned to the youth hostel we were locked out, but the boys managed to climb in through a window and let us in.

After walking into Callander next morning with Ian and Colwyn we parted company, arranging to meet them in Edinburgh on Saturday evening. Jack and Geoff re-joined us and we set off for Dunblane Youth Hostel via Doune. While shopping there we bought milk in cartons, the first I had ever seen. Till then milk was always sold in bottles.

From now on the countryside became less interesting as we left the hills and mountains behind. We saw Stirling castle on our right and passed through Bridge of Allan to Alloa for refreshment, on through Clackmannan, Curnock and Dunfermline, and headed southwards to North Queensferry. We crossed the River Forth by ferry alongside the famous bridge and had tea at South Queensferry. From the outskirts of Edinburgh we had a glimpse of the city, but had to press on along cobbled roads to Kingsknowe where we found the youth hostel.

An early bus into Edinburgh on Saturday morning soon had us spending what money we had left on presents and souvenirs. We had dinner and looked round the gardens in Princes Street before walking up to the castle for a wonderful view over the city. In the evening we met Ian and Colwyn who showed us the old part of the town – St. Giles, The Royal Mile, Holyrood Palace, Heriots and one old road full of ancient houses and fourteen pubs. After coffee in a café, they returned us to the youth hostel.

We had cycled 340 Scottish miles in two weeks, but not cycling every day, and it was time to return home. Our train left Edinburgh at 9:30 am, but we were delayed for 2 hours at Carlisle because of a derailment. On arriving at Trent Junction where we changed again, Barbara and I each had 4d left (old money). After a cup of tea each she had 1d and I had 2 halfpennies! The boys had been thriftier! It had been an epic journey which we had all enjoyed tremendously.

Back at work things carried on as normal for the rest of the year.

Chapter 9

OH! TO BE TWENTY SOMETHING (1951-1952)

During the winter of 1951 we stayed in some of Derbyshire's youth hostels, trudging through the snow on foot.

In the spring I had further veterinary training at the Vet Lab in Weybridge and at Whitsun we did more youth hostelling on bikes in Lincolnshire and Leicestershire.

My summer holiday was two weeks in Jersey in June along with my friend Madge and her friend Olive. We stayed at the Sunshine Hotel in St. Helier which was full of young people about our own age. The sun shone for the whole two weeks. We had tremendous fun.

Some days a coach took us to a variety of sandy bays where we swam and played all kinds of games and sports on the beach. Equipment was supplied by the hotel. We visited sights such as the German Underground Hospital, Gorey Castle, La Houge Bie etc. At night we danced and had fancy dress competitions. The weather was extremely hot and we came home very tanned, but we had been on the go all the time, no lying around sunbathing.

In December my brother Harry married Jean at St. Martin's church in Sherwood and I was a bridesmaid. We had Christmas dinner at the Flying Horse as usual.

When 1952 arrived I had a week's holiday still to take, so Barbara and I stayed at the youth hostel in Central London and went to concerts and the theatre, and of course did plenty of sightseeing and shopping. Then at Easter we got on our bikes again and cycled to our favourite youth hostel – Houghton Mill near Huntingdon, also pulling in stopovers at Whissendine, Ely and King's Cliffe hostels. In those days it was quite safe to cycle down the A1 as there was very little traffic. At Houghton Mill we watched the water rushing down the mill-race beneath our feet as we stood cooking breakfast. Afterwards we paddled canoes in the mill pond.

Many years later I took Dick to visit the mill as it is still operational. When we reached the top floor, a steward asked if we had been before. "Yes," I said, "I slept in this room several times when it was a youth hostel, and in the mornings we used to sweep the dust through a hole in the floor into the boys' dormitory!"

In June that year I was invited to go on a two-week holiday with Madge and her parents – Mr & Mrs Perkins. They had always been very kind to me and treated me like a second daughter. I had enjoyed many a trip out in their car on a Sunday afternoon so this invitation sounded exciting. We were going to Tenby in Pembrokeshire. Our journey took us through much of the Welsh countryside, stopping occasionally at small market towns where there were often sheep fairs or markets. There seemed to be sheep everywhere, an animal of which I am particularly fond. We went through mountain passes and saw huge waterfalls and still more sheep on the hills. Yes! This was my sort of countryside.

Tenby was lovely. Our hotel overlooked the little harbour from where we had boat rides. At 7am some mornings I would go down to the harbour to watch the monks from Caldey Island unload their farm produce. We were able to visit Caldey and see the monks at work in the fields. A long, cobbled road with hedges of fuchsia either side led up to a beautiful chapel with a cobbled floor, but only men were allowed to go into the monastery. It was a lovely, peaceful island. We visited Manorbier and Carew Castles, Pembroke Docks where we saw flying boats, and the lovely water-lily beds at Bosherston. All along the coast were pretty villages like Saundersfoot, Lydstep, Pendine Sands (sand yacht racing), St. Govan's Chapel (down precarious steps in the rocks) and many more places of interest. We still found time to swim in the sea every day.

Then it was back to work until Christmas when once again the Flying Horse was our venue for Christmas dinner.

In our 20s we spent a lot of time dancing, especially on Saturday evenings when we often went to Gilbert's on Mapperley Plains. There were usually plenty of partners available.

Chapter 10

NORWAY (1953)

My summer holiday for 1953 had been planned and booked before Dick and I started courting, so it was Barbara and I who set off on another youth hostelling holiday to Norway. This time without our bikes, as we had been told the route we had planned had very rough roads. So we hiked!

We took the train from Nottingham to Newcastle on July 3rd and boarded the ferry boat M.S. Venus for the overnight crossing to Bergen. We had a very comfortable cabin and a substantial evening meal and a wonderful breakfast from their 'Smorgasbord' – a kind of self-service bar. We noticed that Norwegians had very big appetites!

On arrival in Bergen next morning, our first task was to find the youth hostel, so we asked a policeman on 'point duty' (these were always to be found in any country at busy junctions, before the days of traffic lights). He pointed to the top of the funicular railway so off we went. This was Mount Floyen – 1,000 feet. There was a magnificent view from the top in all directions, but looking over the city and the harbour with its fish and flower markets and the coloured houses of Bryggen was spectacular. That evening we sat up on the hillside in the dusk enjoying the view and getting very badly bitten by mosquitos. In fact, we were so badly bitten that the next morning we went to a small hospital to get the bites treated. We then went in search of the famous Fantoft Stavkirke – a typical Norwegian Church built entirely of wood inside and out (it burnt down several years ago but was quickly re-built).

The next day Barbara decided the home of Grieg at Troldhaugen was a 'must see', so we caught a small train to Hop and walked by the lake to this beautiful spot. The house full of treasures was well worth the visit. (I have been again in recent years and there is now a concert hall built in 1985 with wonderful acoustics). We visited the harbour-side markets in Bergen and lots of lovely shops. We explored the overhanging houses in the Hanseatic Quarter and the colourful houses of Bryggen on the waterfront.

After three nights in Bergen, we took the train to Voss where we spent some time in the town, and then headed out to the youth hostel in semi-darkness and low cloud. It wasn't until the next morning that we realised there was a huge mountain just outside our window. There were youngsters from other Scandinavian countries staying there, but we managed some conversation and then had a sing-song led by a very friendly warden. Meals had been pre-booked at most hostels so we didn't have to cook. However, our next hostel was in a private house well off the beaten track with no food provided. It was a long trek along the Myrkve Valley, so we had an alfresco meal on the roadside near Vinje where we had just bought milk at a dairy and provisions from a small shop. I soon had our little frying pan on our very small solid-fuel cooker, when along came a lone Cambridge student aiming for the overnight accommodation. He accompanied us most of the way.

The youth hostel was a smart, typical Norwegian wooden chalet-type house. On the beds were duvets – something neither of us had ever seen before! The owners didn't speak any English but made us very welcome and insisted that the kitchen was ours to use as and when we wished. We cooked more food that evening and again in the morning, but had to leave early to catch the only daily bus back to the main road. More miles on foot took us to the top of the Naeroydal Canyon, where stands the famous Stalheim Hotel. We spoke to a couple in their 60s who said they wished they had done as we were doing whilst they were young. They were staying at the hotel and took us in for coffee. We were then taken out the rear of the hotel to see the wonderful view down the canyon. (42 years later I returned to this hotel on a coach holiday. The original hotel had burnt down and had been re-built and was much bigger with a large shop selling all kinds of Norwegian goodies).

Our route lay through the canyon, but there were 16 zig-zags of steep mountainside to negotiate before we reached the bottom. (So glad we left the bikes at home!) Then on a few more miles before we reached the ferry at Gudvangen, but the driver of an empty bus picked us up for the last mile or two. The ferry took us through Naeroyfjord and Aurlandfjord where we saw a farmstead with hay drying on lines – lots of it, and then across Sognfjord to Sogndal where we stayed in the youth hostel after exploring the beautiful surroundings.

The next day the ferry took us to Balestrand for a 3-night stay in the youth hostel. This is a popular holiday spot with the famous Kvikne Hotel on the water's edge. Here we bumped into the couple we had met at Stalheim who again took us into the hotel for coffee. What a privilege this was. During our stay at this lovely spot, we went rowing on the fjord and swam in it - much to the amusement of a bunch of schoolboys. The water was extremely cold!

We took a boat trip to Fjaerland where we saw a wedding party dressed in national costume. We walked to the ice floes from two small glaciers coming down from the Jostedal glacier, the largest in Norway. Here we had a snowball fight with two American girls, Jo and Marion. We sat on a plank bridge and dabbled our feet in the ice-cold water, but not for long!

Another day we took a short ferry ride across the fjord to Vik where there was a 12th century Stave Church. We had to run all the way as the ferry didn't wait long, dumping our backpacks in the hedge bottom to lighten the load.

But when we reached the church, it was locked and we hadn't time to fetch the key from somebody's house. There was also a tiny English church in Balestrand, built of wood in the Stave design. We chose to return to Bergen by sea and were on a slightly smaller boat, which was rather crowded and not very comfortable. I remember standing in the rain on a packed deck near the wheelhouse, where there was a radio with news about the two British spies, Guy Burgess and Donald McLean, who had defected to Russia in 1951. That is my only memory of the rather soggy sea trip back to Bergen.

Two more nights were spent in Bergen and a lot of shopping for souvenirs and presents before embarking on M.S. Leda for the journey home.

1953 ended on a high with Dick and I getting engaged on Christmas Day with lunch at the George Hotel in Nottingham.

Chapter 11

YOUNG FARMERS' CLUB (1953-1954)

GETTING MARRIED (1955)

It was while working at a farm at Wysall, in my job as a Veterinary Assistant, that a family of boys suggested I join the Young Farmers Club. They decided the nearest club to my home was at West Bridgford, so I joined and that was where I was to meet my future husband, Dick. It was quite a large club of about twenty-five members. We met in a room at the library on Friday evenings where we had discussions, visiting speakers and quizzes. Afterwards a few of us invaded a small café nearby where we regularly ordered ham, eggs, chips & peas.

There were outings too – lots of them. When we went to London for the weekend to the Dairy Show we also went to see the West End show called Paint Your Wagon. In springtime a coach load of us visited the Lincolnshire bulb fields.

There were evening visits to farms all over the county often finishing up in the local pub. In winter there were a variety of competitions at county level, where we competed against other YFCs in such things as public speaking, all kinds of competitions and quizzes. These would always finish with a dance.

In January there was the annual County Ball and in May the County Agricultural Show, where we competed in stock judging, poultry dressing, cake making and all manner of other things.

Members of West Bridgford YFC at the Nottinghamshire County Ball 1053

In summer there was usually a seaside outing – Bridlington being the one which stands out in my memory as we had that year begun courting. Ballroom dancing was very popular among Young Farmers, and it was at the dance following a quiz at the Saracen's Head in Southwell that Dick first chose me as his partner. I was delighted, as I had noticed that he was the only lad in our club who could really dance properly and that he had had ballroom lessons. It was January 31st 1953 and it turned out to be a memorable occasion! It was the night of the terrible East Coast floods. When we came out of the hotel it was blowing a gale and pouring with rain. The taxi which five of us had ordered didn't turn up, so we walked to a local garage where we knew they had a taxi, but the proprietor put his head out of the window and declared he wasn't turning out on a "night like this." We all crammed into a local phone box and rang a Nottingham taxi company, who came out to fetch us. Meanwhile Dick had phoned his mother, who told him that the chicken shed roof had blown off! We all got home rather late.

The following Monday we were to meet at the annual Point-to-Point race at Cropwell Bishop to sell programmes, and that evening we danced again in Nottingham. So began our courtship.

In February my friend Marion and I went by train to Taunton to spend a week with my aunt and uncle – Bill and Laurie.

That summer we had lots of YFC farm visits and outings. The most memorable was to Bridlington where I have a photo of Dick standing on his head on the beach. (He had been told he would never be able to do this, as he had had an operation to correct wry neck – torticollis - at the age of three).

We had a day trip by train together to Great Yarmouth. After a lovely day on the beach, we returned to the station about 6pm to see the train 'puffing out'. It took us all night to get home with several changes of train. At 7:30 am I changed into my work clothes and went off to my veterinary job on a farm. I had to keep pricking myself to stay awake. Dick had slept a lot of the way home on the train.

We spent another day visiting Mablethorpe, where Norman & Beryl were on their summer holiday with their children Rosemary and Sally.

At the end of June my friends Marion and David were married at Sutton-on-Trent, and I was a bridesmaid along with Marion's sister Doreen. This was a wonderfully grand occasion with the reception in a marquee on the lawn of the Olde England Hotel.

Soon afterwards in July I went off to Norway with my school friend Barbara for a two-week youth hostelling holiday, leaving Dick behind. I think I sent him a postcard almost every day!

(1954)

Sometime that summer we bought a Bantam Major motorcycle. We went out blackberrying into the Vale of Belvoir and down the Old Fosse Way, nearly to Gloucester. This was then an old unmade road where I had to keep getting off to open the gates. We were also able to visit Keyworth in an evening to see Norman and Beryl and other family.

In the autumn we had a YFC outing to the London Motor Show and we also visited the Ford Works at Dagenham. In November, Dick took me to London again to the Poultry Show and to see Ruby Murray at the theatre. That evening he proposed to me and I accepted! On Christmas Day 1953 we had an engagement dinner party at the George Hotel in Nottingham.

In January 1954 I was required to go and work in Yorkshire for two weeks, which seemed a pity so soon after our engagement, so Dick came up on the motorcycle for the weekend in the middle. Despite the fact that there had been a lot of snow, we managed to get around and do some sight-seeing. As I didn't know the area, the heavy snow posed problems for me getting about and finding farms I needed to visit. Some were quite isolated and at one which was about half-a-mile from the road and a very basic farmhouse, I had to cross a bridge over the stream to use the 'privy' on the other side.

At Easter we visited Matlock and Dovedale. We also rode out to Staythorpe to visit Dick's Uncle Wilfred and Auntie Muriel. This we were able to do more often now we had the motorbike. In May we had yet another YFC outing to New Brighton.

Our summer holiday was to Guernsey in the Channel Islands where we stayed in a hotel in St. Peter Port. While there we visited Sark, a small island without motor cars. Transport was (and still is) by horse and cart or tractor and trailer. We really fell in love with Sark, it was so quiet and peaceful. We also spent a day on the tiny island of Herm where there is a famous shell beach and not a lot else. We liked the Channel Islands so much we planned to spend our honeymoon in Jersey. We also dreamed of buying a farm there, but that remained just a dream.

As we both had another week of holiday, we decided to explore the parts of Hampshire where Dick grew up. So we booked into a hotel in Southsea. He then showed me most of Portsmouth where he was living and working when the war started. We visited his friend Eric Slape who had a fish shop, and with whom he used to go sea fishing in Portsmouth harbour and the Solent. We also looked up Dick's parents' good friends, the Greens, who lived at Porchester. I am still in touch with their daughter. As we were so close it was an ideal opportunity to visit the Isle of Wight for a couple of days which we did.

The most memorable visit was to Meonstoke in the Meon Valley where Dick grew up and went to the village school. His family had lived in two different houses and he had been a choirboy in the church at Exton. We went for a walk up a very picturesque track at the back of Exton village that the locals called 'Little Switzerland'. It is such a lovely area. We were still going there frequently, sixty years later!

The early part of 1955 went in a flash with preparations for our wedding on May 19th. As we had no resident vicar at St. Martin's at Sherwood at the time, we decided to get married at Keyworth where Dick lived, and asked Marion's husband David Smith if he would marry us in the chapel there. This he did with the help of the local minister. We held the reception at the Trent

Bridge Inn (TBI) – a hotel which was very popular at the time. As the wedding was on a Thursday, we spent our first night in London at the Strand Palace Hotel and our second night on the ferry to Jersey, where we stayed for a week at the Portelet Hotel on a promontory looking out to sea.

After the honeymoon we returned to our small cottage in Cotgrave where we lived for almost three years. It was a tied cottage belonging to Dick's Uncle Alan (Margaret and Ruth's father), on whose farm Dick was working.

We straight away began to look for a farm of our own and visited several. Our names were on two lists – one, the Ministry of Agriculture and the other, several County Councils. We qualified for a Ministry of Agriculture smallholding as these had originally been provided for men who had returned from the First War. Now they were becoming available to men from the Second War - Dick being one - and I had worked for the 'Min of Ag' for ten years. We looked at County Council farms in Lincolnshire and Cambridgeshire as well as Nottinghamshire but without success. We were shown Sycamore Farm in Rolleston in 1956 but were told to keep saving!

Two years later we were offered The Croft in Rolleston and accepted it. We moved in on Easter Saturday, April 6th 1958.

Chapter 12

COTGRAVE – OUR FIRST HOME (1955-1957)

Dick was still working on his Uncle Alan's farm, so after our marriage we enjoyed three years in a tied cottage at Cotgrave. It was very basic with two living rooms and three bedrooms. There was no bathroom but there was a bath in the kitchen and a brick copper in the corner, so on bath night we drew the blinds and stoked the fire under the copper and ladled out the water into the bath – great fun. For normal use there was a range in the living room with a small hot water tank to one side. We did have a proper gas cooker. The toilet was a privy down the garden which was emptied regularly by a council lorry. Of course, we always kept a chamber pot under the bed!

In the back garden we grew wonderful vegetables and a long row of lovely sweet peas. Some of the potatoes we grew were big enough to feed us both! I think the garden had been well manured by the previous tenant.

That summer 1955, we got around on the motorbike. We spent a weekend at a country club at Flamborough, we visited Uncle Laurie and Auntie Bill who by then had moved to Slough, we went to John and Marigold's wedding on it, which was held at Eckington near Sheffield, more blackberrying

trips and more YFC visits as well as looking at farms to rent. Our friends Michael and Sylvia Chase bought their first farm at Weston so we visited them from time to time.

In 1956 we went to stay with Barbara and Don at Walmer in Kent and then went back to Jersey for our first wedding anniversary in May. We stayed at the same hotel and even in the same room!

One day that summer Marion's parents, Mr and Mrs Bristow, came to have tea with us and see where we were living. During the course of the visit, I happened to mention that I had received a handsome gift of money from my mother's aunt in America and was thinking of buying a car. Mr Bristow offered me his 'farm car', a Hillman, which I duly purchased.

Now we could take Dick's mother out at weekends and fetch my father to stay with us. I remember going to see the illuminations at Matlock Bath in September and thinking what a wonderful spectacle it was. In November I discovered I was pregnant and gave up my veterinary job. That year we had Christmas dinner at the Flying Horse in Nottingham, which had become one of our favourite haunts, and then spent New Year at Keyworth with Dick's family as usual.

1957 began with a shudder! One morning in January, Dick's brother John had called to see me and we were having coffee in the cottage when there was a noticeable earth tremor. I remember dragging John outside thinking the house was going to collapse. The epicentre was in Charnwood Forest in Leicestershire - not very far away.

Preparations were now in earnest for the arrival of our first baby – Peter, born on June 15th at the Firs maternity home in Sherwood, near to where I had spent the first twenty-six years of my life. It was a lovely summer, and we spent a lot of time in our garden and pushing the pram around the country lanes. In August we took Peter to Walmer in Kent in the Hillman, to visit Barbara and Don and their baby Christopher. In September, we took him to Tenby for a week - he was by now three months old. A week after our return Peter was christened at Cotgrave Church with all the family present. Madge became his Godmother and Harry and Norman his Godfathers. We spent Christmas at Keyworth as usual.

While we were living at Cotgrave I became involved in some local social activities. A lady living in the village taught a variety of crafts in the evenings. The first one I tackled was a basketry course. We tried willow weaving first and I made simple plant holders, trays and then a lovely shopping basket.

Later at the farm I took my eggs to market in it on a regular basis, until one day it was stolen from underneath the stall when empty. Then we did some cane basketry and, after making a few smaller items, I decided to make a cradle for the baby I was expecting. This turned out very well and I won a prize with it. It was used for all three of our baby boys and I used it as a carry cot. It was also used several times at Christmas in our church nativity play. We still have it after more than 60 years. I also joined the village WI and took part in the local amateur dramatics.

Chapter 13

THE CROFT, ROLLESTON

OUR DREAMS COME TRUE (1958-1969)

Early in 1958 we were offered the tenancy of 'The Croft' at Rolleston. We accepted, and moved in on Easter Saturday, 6th April along with our first baby son Peter who was by now nine months old.

The farmhouse was quite large. It had begun life as a one-up, one-down cottage, believed to have once been lived in by a retired coachman of Queen Victoria. It had been extended on either end, one side containing two large living rooms and the other side containing a kitchen, scullery, and two dairies. There were three bedrooms and a toilet upstairs, a bathroom downstairs and also a privy in the garden.

Peter among the chickens before breakfast

My father had lived alone for three years since I married and was lonely, so he came to live with us and was with us for fourteen years. He loved the farm, the garden and the countryside and was very happy.

To begin with we only had fifty-four acres of land where we grew sugar beet and cereals. We bought six cows, a milking machine, a second-hand Ferguson tractor and a trailer with £200.00 left in the bank! Eventually the milking herd increased to seventeen plus followers (beef stock and calves).

The summer of 1958 was rather wet and we found ourselves with a hay crop, which had been cut in July, still standing in the fields in water in September. In fact, on July 2nd the dyke running through our land had flooded and left several inches of water in the fields between the railway line and the Upton boundary. As the steam train on the 'Paddy Line' was still operating, I used to take Peter in the pram on the train to Southwell to the clinic to be weighed etc.

We worked hard as we had no help but we were young (ish) and fit. I had a baby and father to look after and decorating to be done in the house. We were just beginning to get on our feet when in January 1959 we had 'the floods'. At 5am one morning another farmer ran up the village with water following him shouting, "Floods!" By 7am we had moved everything upstairs that could be carried, including carpets which were not fitted in those days. Dick went out to the cattle and put straw bales round the doorways of the sheds. He brought in a can of paraffin and a stove which my uncle had given me. These were used for cooking upstairs for the next eight days. Meanwhile he had found me at the electric cooker in my wellies frying bacon and both sides of a joint of beef which had been delivered that day. He was very cross with me and ripped out the plugs from the electric sockets on the walls which were low down and 'popping'. It was a horrible and frightening experience.

We moved Peter's cot into our bedroom and used his room to live and cook in for a week. The cows had to be milked and all the animals fed. Dick used the tractor to get about.

The milk lorry was unable to reach us for a couple of days so we lost some

milk. Hay and straw stacks soaked up the water so the bottom bales were useless. Cattle feed also got wet. The house had over a foot of water in the main part, but the kitchen, scullery and dairies were much deeper as they were all down steps.

The reason for the flood was that contractors had been building a pipe-line from Staythorpe Power Station to wash ashes to the village of Hoveringham to build breeze blocks for the building industry. When the contractors reached the River Greet on land near the church, they had burst the river bank. The water came down the lane past the church and up the village towards Staythorpe. The houses opposite on Greenaway had flood-water half way up their front paths, but on our side of the road almost every house was affected. As our farmhouse was the lowest lying, we were the last to be pumped out by the fire brigade. When the water had subsided, there was a trail across one room where a newt had been. Dustbins had floated away and discharged their contents all over the village. In the end we were awarded £200 in compensation! And had to start all over again.

Two months after all this I discovered I was pregnant again and then my father was taken ill with a perforated ulcer. After two weeks in hospital, he was taken to a convalescent home at Skegness for two more weeks. This gave me and Peter an excuse for a day at the seaside when we fetched him home.

Later in September I took Peter and Dick's parents to Hoylake on the Wirral Peninsular for a week's holiday. This had been my family's holiday destination when I was a child.

In October we had some re-wiring done in the house and the wooden floors downstairs had to be removed. Cables beneath the floors had been damaged by the floods and the upheaval caused chaos. It was at this time that Peter, now almost two and a half years old, had his first bout of bronchitis. He was really quite poorly and continued to have these periods of illness throughout his young life. I have always suspected that the dampness in the house at this time may have been responsible. Also, he used to touch the damp salty patches on the walls when he was crawling and may have put his fingers in his mouth.

David was born two days before Christmas 1959 in the evening, after I had taken a generous dose of castor oil, "So that we could all have our Christmas dinner in peace," suggested our friendly Dr Savage. I had put up the Christmas Tree and had been making mince pies. The midwife, Nurse Jones, had been doing the same but came as soon as they were cooked. She only just made it. I had the baby without any help. It was a wonderful feeling having the baby so close to Christmas. A teenager from the village, Janet Spinks, came to help Peter decorate the Christmas Tree. My father helped with the cooking; he was quite at home in the kitchen when needed. The doctor called on Christmas Day but as I was asleep he didn't disturb me.

That Christmas we were unable to go to Keyworth as usual, and I decided that thereafter it would be easier for the rest of the family to come to us. So for several years following, we had the Christmas Night party at The Croft.

Often there would be fifteen or twenty of us. On one memorable occasion several years later, the visitors set out for home about midnight and found themselves skidding on black ice on Farndon corner. So they all returned to the farm and we stoked up the fire and made them all comfortable in the sitting room, each with a blanket and footstool. We of course gave them all breakfast and they set off again, this time in daylight.

As far as I remember 1960 was fairly uneventful except that in August, I managed a week's holiday at Cromer with Peter, now 3, David, 9 months and Dick's mother. We had a lovely holiday but it seemed rather tiring up and down stairs at the hotel to change the baby before and after each meal. Up and down the zig-zag cliff path with a pushchair and a toddler, and grandma who had bad legs. Add to that a roof rack where I had to load the luggage myself and all this not realising I was pregnant again.

We celebrated David's first birthday in December and held our first big family party at the farm on Christmas Night.

Early in 1961 we were told by the Ministry of Agriculture that they were going to demolish our farmhouse and build a new house on the same site. Edward was born on May 9th 1961 in the old Croft farmhouse with a midwife in attendance. There was a big family gathering for his christening in August. We didn't manage a holiday that year but we had a lovely hot summer. On September 3rd Harry and Jean and their boys Nigel and Alan came for the day and everyone helped in the harvest field. That night we had the worst thunderstorm I've ever experienced lasting from 10pm until 2am. We discovered later that our neighbours house had been struck by lightning on the corner of the roof.

In November we moved down the road to a vacant property while the old Croft was demolished. From our new abode we saw lorry loads of rubble go past with wallpapered bricks bearing cats and kittens which had been part of the decor in Peter's bedroom. The foundations for the new farmhouse were dug out but, as we had a lot of snow over the Christmas period, they caved in and had to be dug out again in January 1962 – so the date stone on the house is actually incorrect!

That spring we sold our first car (the Hillman) and bought a Ford Squire. In June there was great excitement as we set off on our first seaside holiday as a family. The Clarehaven Hotel at Bognor Regis had been recommended by two of my aunts who had stayed there (Auntie Rita and Auntie Vera), and it welcomed small children and had a baby-listening service in the evenings.

We paid £56 for the five of us for a week (3 star) full board! The waitress who served us, Gwen, had been there 27 years (speaks for itself!) We had booked a beach hut where we left all our gear which proved to be useful. We had a primus stove, kettle etc so that we could make a hot drink. With three small children under five years (two still in high chair and nappies) there was inevitably washing to be done so while Dick supervised their teatime meal, I made use of the laundry room and hung out the washing up on the flat roof of the hotel. It was usually dry by the morning and I could use an iron if necessary.

In July we moved into our new farmhouse. It was much appreciated as it was all newly decorated and much easier to keep clean. The only drawback was the lack of cupboard space, so we went out and bought more wardrobes. That Christmas we had a huge family party round our farmhouse kitchen table, which was replicated for several years to come.

The winter of 1963 was very long and very cold with frost and extremely low temperatures for several weeks. We had many power cuts which not only affected the house but also the farm. Animals were often fed by torchlight and milking was delayed (sometimes halfway through) until power was restored. In early spring, Edward had whooping cough, even though he had been inoculated. He was not yet 2 years old so we had his cot in our bedroom so that we could sit him up when he coughed. A lack of sleep didn't help the workload! We did however manage another holiday at Bognor.

Peter was then at school and contracted mumps in the spring of 1964 passing it on to Edward next. On Good Friday we all went to see Peter Pan at Nottingham Theatre Royal. We shall never forget the exuberant 4-year-old David standing up on his seat and shouting repeatedly, "Go back crocodile!" much to the amusement of most of the audience. The next day he too had mumps and on Easter Sunday I succumbed as well and was quite ill for a week. My father was quite at home in the kitchen when required, and he performed a mammoth task of feeding us all and washing up. (No dishwashers then!)

I had overseen the building of a bungalow in Southwell into which my Godparents from Slough moved during May. For the next twelve years we saw them regularly and they loved being nearer to the family.

Between hay and harvest we had our third holiday at Bognor. Otherwise, farming operations continued 24/7 and there was never a dull moment. The children revelled in the harvest field and in helping to feed the animals. Their cousins visited regularly and envied us our open-air life and the freedom to run around several acres of land and climb trees etc. There was one occasion while the boys were quite young when I was unable to leave them with anybody while I helped Dick drill a field of corn. So they stood on a bar behind the drill with me to make sure the seed ran freely into the coulters. They loved it! (It would be illegal nowadays). When I put them in the bath later that evening, David was covered in chicken pox!

We spent a few summer nights camping in the field furthest from the farmhouse. The boys revelled in this. We had an old family tent that had belonged to Dick's Uncle Alan and had been well used for many years. It was pitted with tiny holes where he had disposed of moths with a candle so it leaked a bit when it rained. There was no flysheet! We cooked our breakfast on a primus stove at daybreak while the birds were singing, and then walked across the fields back home to feed the animals and milk the cows. I remember hearing a corncrake at night and we regularly heard and saw skylarks during the day.

As Peter's birthday is in June, he often had a cowboy party in a field full of hay bales. His friends came dressed as cowboys with their toy guns (every little boy had one in those days). I would drive the car across the fields to them with the picnic tea and bottles of lemonade. They never wanted to go home!

At the age of eight Peter drove the tractor in the field sometimes. But then when he was thirteen a new law forbade this until the age of fourteen so he had a frustrating one-year ban.

In 1965 Peter joined Southwell Cub Scouts and paraded through the town on St. George's Day for the first time. We had our fourth holiday at Bognor, and from there the boys and I went on to stay with Barbara and her three boys at Deal in Kent for a further week, while Dick came home on the train. While on the beach at Sandwich Bay we had a scary moment when David got stuck in quicksand whilst in the sea and we had to pull him out.

The following year, 1966, Dick was invited to a special service at Westminster Abbey for recipients of the Military Medal. This happened to fall on his birthday and he was able to take me and the boys along too. The parade and salute took place in Dean's Yard at 4pm, followed by the service. We went off early by train from Newark so that we could spend the day sightseeing. It was July and very warm, so we left our coats in a locker at King's Cross station rather than carry them around all day. We had a good day and made our way to Dean's Yard just before 4pm. As soon as everyone had assembled for the parade the heavens opened and the rain came down like stair rods. In no time at all we were all soaked (and in our best clothes too). We sat through the service in the Abbey literally steaming. It was still raining when we came out so we headed for the nearest café for some tea. While there the rain stopped and we walked back to the station in bright sunshine. We retrieved our coats and caught the train home.

Bognor was on the agenda again in August, followed by another week at Deal.

In the spring of 1967, I did a week-long Gardeners' Course at Brackenhurst, our local Horticultural College as it was then. At Whitsuntide (now called Spring Bank Holiday), we held our first Church Flower Festival at Rolleston, which became an annual event, though later changed to Easter weekend. I had joined the local Women's Institute and in June was asked to represent them at the National AGM at the Royal Albert Hall.

We had our sixth holiday at Bognor and on the journey home called and spent the afternoon with Don, Pat and family in their beautiful garden at Virginia Water. They called their lovely house 'Merry Tilers' because the men who tiled the roof sang all the while they were working. In the autumn we went to the village of Norwell to watch a spectacular 'Son et Lumière' which was projected onto the outside of their church during darkness. It was unique to this area and brilliantly displayed.

1968 was quite a busy year. The Sunday School put on an Epiphany Pageant which was well supported. At Easter, Peter went to Swanage in Dorset with Lowes Wong School. In May David joined Bleasby Cub Scouts because he knew there would be Sea Scouts to follow. There was a Sunday School outing to Drayton Manor Park and a Natter Club visit to Averham Theatre to see Charley's Aunt.

Some of the Mums and Babes in the Natter Club

We held another Church Flower Festival at Rolleston in June and went off to Bognor for two weeks in August. In November I went with my friend Sylvia to Denman College near Abingdon for a week's tailoring course where I made a tweed suit (this is a WI college). Just before Christmas I took the boys back south to Frances and Ron's wedding at Chichester.

In 1969 the boys and I had an enjoyable week in the Lake District staying at Dale Bottom Farm near Keswick. As this area was new to them, we toured round in the car stopping frequently to explore. We did a lot of hill walking including Cat Bells and we walked right around Lake Buttermere and climbed a big waterfall. We picnicked most days, washing our pots and pans in mountain streams. Bed and breakfast at the farm cost us just £12.00. Most evenings were spent dancing in the barn. We paid our eighth visit to Bognor in August in our old Austin A40, which we had acquired from Aunt Edith. We brought home a quarter-size, slate-bed, Riley snooker table on the roof rack of the car. It took six men to lift it on! This had been offered to us the previous year by Mr Dryden, the manager of the hotel, but we had no roof rack then. En route home we stopped off at Kidlington near Oxford to attend the wedding of Dick's niece Rosemary and her husband Pete. The snooker table was quite a talking point.

Chapter 14

OBERAMMERGAU & JOINING THE SEA SCOUTS

(1970-1976)

After eight years in a row spending our summer holiday at Bognor while the boys were young, we decided to take them abroad in alternate years. So in 1970 we booked to go to see the world famous Passion Play in Oberammergau in Germany. In order to fulfil Dick's wish to see some of his wartime battlefields restored to normality, we planned to camp there and back.

We took the ferry from Harwich to Ostend and found our first campsite at Lac Loppen just as it was getting dark. Some kind Belgian campers helped us put up our family tent and made us a hot drink. The next day we stopped to have a look at Ghent and Bruges and I remember seeing overhead traffic lights for the first time. We had a picnic lunch by the river and then pressed on to our next campsite at Dendremonde. This was a small site with a pond and some waterfowl. A swan sat on its large nest right next to the toilet block, complaining whenever we approached and making us rather cautious.

We crossed the border into Germany in the morning showing our passports to the guards. After crossing the rather superior new bridge at Bonn, we followed the River Rhine south to Bad Godesburg where we appeared to camp in somebody's back garden! Further south we found the river in flood and our chosen campsite at Lahnstein under water. We decided to drive up to Oberlahnstein where there was a very cold swimming pool on the campsite, so cold that only David braved a brief swim. En route to our next campsite, having left the Rhine, we drove into Karlsrhuhe, which years later became twinned with Nottingham and where local farmers made exchange visits. That evening found us near Ulm beside a large lake with hire boats, and we pitched our tent on a hillside full of fruit trees with blossom falling all over us.

No-one was allowed to camp at Oberammergau while the play was on, so we had booked accommodation in a lovely chalet bungalow where we had bed and breakfast. All other meals were provided at a hotel where we ate at the same table for each meal. It was all extremely well organised. We arrived on the 2nd June, saw the play on the 3rd and left the town on the 4th. The Passion Play was fabulous. Actors, costumes, scenery (the backdrop was the actual mountain behind the stage) were all of the highest quality. It was all in German and we had a German script. Provided one knew the story of Holy Week and the Crucifixion it was easy to follow, our boys were only 12, 10 and 9 years old, but they understood it. The German language isn't unlike our own, as I found out years later at evening classes.

We set off for our next campsite on a farm at Untersteinbach having crossed the border into Austria briefly. Here we had a bit of a scare as the border guards were in their hut, and Dick drove straight by the free-standing barrier thinking it was road works, as he hadn't realised where we were. The guards ran after us shouting at us to "Stop!" with hands on their gun holsters. We reversed back up to them and wound down the window. "Sorry," said Dick in a very British accent as they rolled their eyes. We apologised and showed our passports and they let us go. It all added to the excitement, especially for the boys.

For the next 2 nights we camped near Meersburg on the side of Lake Geneva, with steam trains running just behind us. We took a ferry and crossed the lake into Switzerland for the afternoon, so that we could say our holiday took us into six different countries. On Sunday morning I was driving in Luxembourg city and went the wrong way down a main street. Luckily it was not very busy!

We spent our last two nights in Northern France on a rather noisy campsite. We were very close to a canal where heavy barges drum! drum! drummed! by us all night long. We were sleeping on the ground so the noise reverberated. The other side of us was a large pond full of frogs which croaked all night, and at about 3am a couple in a nearby caravan had a blazing row – in French of course!

The in-between day was spent searching for the grave of my Uncle Harry who was killed in the First World War. After looking in a couple of War Cemeteries unsuccessfully, we found his grave in the village cemetery at Bethune. Here the gardener showed us Harry's name in the Book of Remembrance, insisted we all sign the visitors book and then showed us to the grave, which was immaculately kept and surrounded by flowering rockery plants. We took photos as no-one else in our family had ever visited the grave. (His name is on the War Memorial at Nottingham High School, St. Andrew's Church and now the new memorial on the River Trent Embankment.) We returned home by hovercraft from Dieppe to Newhaven.

That summer there were visits to Harrogate, Rugby, the Wedgewood factory and York Minster. David joined the 6th Newark Sea Scouts, which was the beginning of our family's connection with Sea Scouts for about 20 years. The worst day of the year was still to come. On a Saturday in October, Dick found the haystack on fire. Two fire brigades attended from Newark and Southwell and remained for over 12 hours. Local farmers brought their tractors and front loaders and pulled apart some of the burning hay and straw and spread it on the adjacent field in heaps, where it smouldered for two weeks. We were insured but we had spent many hours and lots of effort loading and unloading and stacking all those hundreds of bales.

In February 1971 my father (Pop as he was known to the family) celebrated his 80th birthday with an 'open house' day, when family and friends popped in throughout the day for a drink and a bite to eat. He seemed very well despite having had surgery in December and he loved having the family around him.

David (always the ambitious one) began piano lessons at home with a new tutor. This was the Beatles era which must have shaped his lifelong love of music. He bought a guitar and taught himself to play it, and in later years played many local gigs and wrote music and lyrics too.

In May I took the boys camping at Stratford-upon-Avon, Cheddar Gorge and Weymouth. We visited Shakespeare's birthplace, Cheddar Caves, Portland Lighthouse, Chesil Beach and the Bovington Tank Museum. The rest of the week was spent in the sea as the weather was very hot. In July the whole family spent a week at Bognor for the ninth time. August brought David's first Scout camp which was beside Bassenthwaite Lake in the Lake District. I was invited to stay in a caravan nearby with the wives of two Scout leaders and their small children, and to take Edward with me. We joined in some of their activities such as hiking through Borrowdale, climbing Skiddaw and Cat Bells, and I did some canoeing on the lake and on the sea at St. Bees. When we returned home, I was invited to join 6th Newark Sea Scouts as an assistant leader. This was the start of my own involvement with the Sea Scouts which lasted over fifteen years (I had already helped with two Cub Packs for nearly five years).

In November, sadly, Pop died and this left a big gap in the family, as he had lived with us at the farm for fourteen years since Peter, our first-born, was nine months old. So he had watched all the boys grow up and enjoyed helping and playing with them while they were young. He had loved living on the farm with us, and had his own patch of garden where he spent a lot of his time. He always washed the tea pots while I put the boys to bed which was a great help. He also liked sawing logs and chopping sticks for the fire. He would accompany me to school to watch the boys' various activities. We all missed him very much.

In 1972 Scouting activities predominated. There were canoe slaloms on the River Trent at Newark Town Lock in spring and autumn, and another one at Peterborough one very cold weekend in November. We took part in the Sea Scout Trophy at Barton Island on the River Trent near Attenborough. Here, each summer, Sea Scout troops from the area gathered for a weekend camping and participating in a variety of challenges and competitions. These included sailing, canoeing, gig pulling (a crew of four in a heavy type of rowing boat, each with one oar to pull) and 'sculling over the stern', where one competitor stood alone in the stern of a small boat with a single oar sited on the stern, and by moving the oar in a figure of eight in the water could propel the boat forwards. It was a tricky manoeuvre and required lots of practice! In addition to boating there was rope work and knots, tent pitching, orienteering, and questions on 'rules of the road' for boats etc. Points were scored and a trophy awarded. This weekend was one of the highlights of the year for me and many of the Scouts, though not everyone took part.

The favourite activity for most Scouts was the Summer Camp which was always well attended. Usually, we found a private site near water and within reach of the hills and the mountains, so that the boys could take part in a variety of activities. If at all possible, we preferred a farm where we were allowed to cook on wood fires. We were noted for our Sunday roast cooked in a homemade oven below ground – with a chimney! This particular summer we camped at Gellylliden near Portmadoc in North Wales. In addition to canoeing on the sea and river estuary, we climbed a mountain called Moel Siabod and visited the slate village of Blaenau Ffestiniog by way of the narrow-gauge railway. My abiding memories of this camp were of the sheep bleating nearly all night long, and of singing round the camp fire the current popular songs, 'We All Live in a Yellow Submarine' by the Beatles and 'Where Have All the Flowers Gone' by Peter, Paul and Mary.

During the year the boys and I joined the North Notts Canoe Club along with two other Sea Scout leaders and some of the older and more proficient Scouts. We camped for long weekends at Black Rock Sands near Portmadoc and also Bamburgh opposite the Farne Islands on the Northumbrian coast. We also canoed at Wells-next-the-Sea in Norfolk among other venues.

Our family holiday in 1972 was ten days on the coast of Normandy at Houlgate. We crossed the channel from Harwich to Ostend and drove down the coast visiting Etretat, Honfleur and Deauville en route. Of course we camped! I remember seeing glow-worms all around the tent at night. We visited Pegasus Bridge and the museum and then went to Arromanches to visit the museum there. We returned home by hovercraft from Calais to Ramsgate (we used the hovercraft on several occasions and were disappointed when the service stopped).

Dick went to Germany with a party of local farmers. They stayed in Karlsruhe which is twinned with Nottingham. Whilst there they visited the Unimog factory, and attended other events that had been put on for them. I began teaching at the Sunday School in Rolleston and we put on our first Christmas play of many. It had been another very busy year.

It was because Peter had left school and was working on the farm that I was able to carry out these voluntary activities, but I still helped with hay and harvest and looked after the chickens and the garden with its plentiful crops of fruit and vegetables.

At Spring Bank Holiday weekend of 1973, we took a party of Scouts to the Biblins log cabin in the Wye Valley where we canoed on the River Wye (tackling the white water), and we visited Monmouth and Tintern Abbey. Everyone took part in night hikes in the Forest of Dean, as always using only a map and compass. (No mobile phones or GPS in those days!)

Our Summer Camp in August was at Botley in Hampshire where I took on the role of Assistant Quartermaster. With thirty Scouts in camp this was a necessary and rewarding job which I really enjoyed. We had taken the pulling boat and several canoes which were well used on the local river and on the sea at Hayling Island. But for me the highlight of the week was a visit to the Royal Navy in Portsmouth. Here we were invited to visit Whale Island where the Gunnery School is situated at HMS Excellent. We were shown the new Exocet missile and everyone had a turn on the Seacat missile simulator. The boys were then dressed in full waterproofs, and took turns at loading blank shells into a heavy gun on a moving platform simulating a rough sea. Suddenly they were drenched with water from above but continued loading. They loved it! The leaders looked on from a dry balcony.

Flag Break at Botley camp 1975

At lunch time the Scouts ate in the Ratings' Mess but we leaders were invited to the Officers' Mess. Here we had 'silver service' and a fabulous meal. Geoff was asked to roll his shirt sleeves down! There had been a hiccup over my hat. I was wearing a Wren's flat hat with a Scout Badge on it. Under no circumstances could it be seen hanging in the entrance to the Officers' Mess along with the men's caps, so it was hidden away while we had lunch. Later while we were watching a parade, they insisted on sending someone into Portsmouth to buy me a Wren Officer's hat.

Next, we were taken by coach to the end of the Whale Island peninsular where we were instructed in letting off distress flares. We stood well back in a row, as each individual stepped forward alone to release their flare. I was invited to go first being the only female. Gosh! What power they have, I really thought my arm had gone with it. They were all out of date but they all worked! It had been an exciting and interesting day and may well have encouraged some of the Scouts to join the Royal Navy, as did our middle son David who was then thirteen. We returned to Portsmouth another day, to visit HMS Victory and have a boat trip round the harbour, some Scouts having a chance to steer the boat.

Soon after the Summer Camp the 6th Newark Sea Scouts applied for Admiralty Inspection and were awarded a prestigious place in a list of selected Sea Scout Troops. Standards had to be maintained and the Troop was inspected every year. I believe it still is.

In October we took part in the National Sea Scout Regatta at Holme Pierrepont on the outskirts of Nottingham. Sea Scouts came from all over the country to compete in sailing, canoeing, rowing etc. for a number of national trophies. As there were a large number of competitors and Scouts had to wait between heats, I organised a 'BAT polo' competition. There were a dozen short, blunt-ended BAT canoes available so we had 6-a-side water polo matches. All this happened several years running in October, and at the end of one Sunday afternoon, as they were loading up to go home, a leader from Southampton offered me six BAT canoes for £25. I snapped them up and 6th Newark had years of fun with them, especially canoe surfing on the sea.

During the winter of 1973, 6th Newark Scouts hired the Grove Swimming Pool at Balderton on Saturday mornings for canoe training – it was basically a 'drown-proofing' course, to teach the Scouts how to escape from an upturned canoe! It was very successful. Some of the older boys even learned to do the 'Eskimo roll' in their canoes (this rights the canoe without getting out), a technique which I found hard to master, but which was easier to learn in a swimming pool than in the rough waters of the River Trent slalom course. We took a party of Scouts to the Earl's Court Boat Show at London and the Nottingham Gang Show at the Nottingham Theatre Royal. After seeing this, 6th Newark Sea Scouts decided to have a go at presenting our own small show at Newark Palace Theatre. I had heard on the radio a school programme called 'Mutiny on the Cutty Sark'. The songs and the script seemed appropriate for Sea Scouts so I wrote to the BBC and got permission to use them. We were not allowed to use the word 'Gang' as the show didn't contain a large enough percentage of Ralph Reader material – the fellow who wrote and produced the national Gang Shows. With the help of another Scout leader, who had some previous experience, we produced 'Under Sail' with huge success and put in a few short 'turns' including a humorous rendering of The Owl and the Pussycat, with appropriate props. We made a huge banner advertising the show which was strung above and across Appletongate in the centre of Newark. It was a fantastic experience and everybody seemed to enjoy it.

In 1974 apart from scouting, we all enjoyed Sally's wedding at Kidlington on Valentine's Day. Also in February, Dick went on a four-day visit to Belgium with a group of farmers, looking at Belgian farming methods. At Easter we held another Rolleston Church Flower Festival.

During the school holidays I took a party of Scouts to South Wales for five days. We stopped in an old Miners' Welfare Centre, Pwll Dhu, in the foothills of the mountains near Abergavenny. It had been converted into a youth activity centre and was well off the beaten track. We spent our time hill walking and orienteering.

In June Dick paid his first visit to Normandy since the war, with his army comrades. I had to stay and look after the farm! This was the first visit of many and saw the unveiling and dedication of the memorial to the 11th Armoured Division, just outside the town of Flers. This had been the first large town the 11th Armoured Division had liberated after D-Day. Over the next thirty years Dick and I made another dozen or so visits to the area. Most were organised events which included a service at the memorial on the Sunday morning, followed by a banquet in one of the local villages or the Château at Flers. On every occasion everybody was hosted by a French family. On my first visit in 1981 we stayed with the widow of the local judge at Montamy. She didn't speak English so we had to manage with my schoolgirl French. This soon returned and developed tremendously over the years. The family had had General Montgomery's caravan in their garden after the liberation, and there were bullet holes in their front door.

On our next visit in 1984 we were hosted by Jean and Monique Martin and their family at Cahagnes. We became great friends and over the years have visited them more than a dozen times. They also visited us while we were at the farm and also in our present home. My French continues to improve as they do not speak English (more of these visits later).

Our family holiday in 1974 was spent camping in Jersey for two weeks. We took the car across so that we could explore the island. The weather was extremely hot to begin with, reaching 98 degrees F and 86 degrees F some days, so we spent most of the time in the sea or the swimming pool. On our return I spent a week at Gilwell Park in Essex, the International Headquarters of Scouting, doing the Advanced Leader Training Course along with 44 male leaders. I was told that I was the first female Sea Scout Leader in the country.

We were put into Patrols as the Scouts are and I am still in touch with my Patrol Leader from Solihull. We took part in a variety of activities as well as classroom training sessions. But the highlight of my week was the building of a rope bridge across to an island in an old bomb crater. Only one person was allowed to get wet so, as I had my wetsuit in my car - guess who that was!

89

We certainly learned how to tie reliable knots. By the end of the week we had all earned our 'Wood Badge', the symbol of which is a row of wooden beads similar to the ones worn by the Matabeles in the Boer War, worn around the neck with a special neckerchief. As we departed for home, the District Commissioner for Columbo in Sri Lanka invited me to take my family for a holiday on the shores of their beautiful island. Sadly, I had to decline as we were still very busy farming.

Next was our annual Summer Scout Camp, this year on a farm near St. Austell in Cornwall. It was an unusually big camp with Cubs, Scouts and Venture Scouts, and it took a lot to organise the activities to suit all the different age groups. The Scouts managed a visit to the Royal Navy at Plymouth and we hiked on Exmoor. Soon after our return we held a big ceremony for the opening of the 6th Newark Sea Scout compound on the riverside at Farndon. It was and still is a fantastic facility with full access to the River Trent.

In October I was invited to become Sea Scout Leader of 1st Farndon Group, who had recently been changed to Sea Scouts and, apart from everyone having new uniforms, had purchased a number of canoes and a pulling boat together with all the necessary equipment. The Leaders had left and the Group was threatened with closure unless a new Leader could be found. This was a wonderful challenge which I accepted and stayed as Leader for twelve years. I started with sixteen Scouts whose number increased to twenty-six at one point, so we were never a large Troop like 6th Newark, but we entered all the competitions and even won some. The Scouts enjoyed coming to the farm to camp on numerous occasions, and learnt many skills such as axemanship, camp cooking, rope work and orienteering.

In the spring of 1975, and now Leader of 1st Farndon Sea Scouts, we again visited the Biblins log cabin in the Wye Valley, took part in the canoe slalom at Newark Town Lock, erected a large flagpole at the Newark and Notts County Show and took part in the Sea Scout Trophy at Barton Island. We had an early camp, returning to Botley in Hampshire from where we visited HMS Daedalus after whom the Troop was named. This is a shore-based Royal Navy Air Station at Lee-on-the-Solent and was a Search and Rescue Centre for part of the south coast. The Royal Navy had planned to take us up in a helicopter but received a call-out while we were there. Unfortunately we never did get to go up in a helicopter. However, we did get to watch the teams practicing for the Royal Tournament – taking apart the field guns and putting them back together again. It was a race against the clock and appeared quite dangerous. Several ratings had injuries and one suffered a broken arm.

In July we had our eleventh holiday at Bognor Regis, taking with us our friends Mary, Alan and their daughter Julie, plus the small boat that Alan had built with David and of course my canoe. As usual we spent most of the week in the sea.

The reason for holding an early Scout Camp that year was because I was trying to organise a trip to Norway in July/August, in order to visit the World Scout Jamboree at Lillehammer. In the end only six people from Newark were able to go, so we joined up with 3rd Woodthorpe and 1st Redhill Scout Troops in Nottingham. My nephew Tony had told me there were some vacant seats on their coach so we jumped at the idea.

This was a highly organised camp with Cubs, Scouts and Venture Scouts. We hired a coach and a large van to take the equipment plus some canoes, and one Leader took his family with their camper van. We crossed by ferry from Newcastle to Bergen where a meal had been arranged for us, before driving through the night to our campsite at Gol, halfway between Bergen and Oslo, next to a fast-flowing river with rapids. There was an extensive choice of activities both on and off camp, from canoeing to mountaineering and hiking in the forests, where some Scouts camped overnight. It had rained heavily all day and night and was doing so when we arrived at about 2am, thankful that some Norwegian Scouts had already pitched our tents for us. When we awoke at 7am the sun was shining and did so every day for the two weeks we were there.

The highlight of the camp was on Friday at the end of the first week, when we all piled into the coach early in the morning and set off for Lillehammer. After stopping at a railway café for breakfast, we reached the Jamboree in good time and were able to spend about 6 – 7 hours there. We found the one Scout from Newark who had been allocated a place there (remember, no mobile phones in those days) and we spoke with Scouts from all over the world, exchanging lots of badges with them. There were also many activities we could all join in.

Around 6pm we re-joined our coach and drove in the direction of Oslo, stopping at a restaurant en route where an evening meal had been booked for us all. Then we went on to Oslo where we had arranged to stay in a large Scout House for two nights. Saturday was spent sight- seeing in Oslo, visiting the Viking ships, the Kon–Tiki and the Fram. We took a train to Hohenkollen and walked up the famous ski jump. Some people chose to visit the Vigeland Statue Park while others went shopping. On Sunday we returned to Gol for our second week and after that back to Bergen, where we had time to do more sight-seeing before embarking on the ferry back to Newcastle.

Scouting continued apace for the rest of the year, with a Leaders' re-union at Gilwell Park at the beginning of September and a rather scary canoe trip later in the month. I had planned to canoe from Fiskerton to Farndon on the River Trent with six of our more canoe-proficient Scouts. We set off at 2pm in fine weather but within fifteen minutes it began to rain, gently at first but then more and more heavily. All was well until the wind increased and, as we rounded a bend in the river, we were met with really strong gusts and waves. One by one the Scouts began to capsize but we righted them and carried on until it was my turn to get a soaking. It was then that I decided to abandon the trip as it was becoming dangerous. Unfortunately, we were at a point where the river is at its furthest from any village, so we had to carry and drag our canoes across fields. It was a relief to get home!

[That particular night, 28th September 1975, was the night of a tragic accident at Cromwell Weir just downstream from Newark on the River Trent. Royal Engineers regiment sappers, of Grangemouth, Falkirk, were on an 80-mile night-time exercise, when the motor boats they were in unwittingly went over the weir and capsized. Ten soldiers lost their lives and one survived, in what remains the 131st Independent Parachute Squadron's largest peacetime tragedy. Conditions had been worsened by the bad weather and a high tide at Cromwell.]

I was glad we had abandoned our canoe trip when we did!
In December we put on a four-night Gang Show at Newark Palace Theatre. I helped to produce the District Cubs contribution of 'Snow White and the 77 Dwarfs'.

1976 was rather a sad year as we lost two aunts, two uncles and a very close friend. But farming continued apace, and now Peter was working on the farm alongside Dick and therefore my help was not required on a regular basis, but always of course at hay time and harvest. The dairy herd had been sold as we had great difficulty getting the cows across the railway line which ran through our fields. Trains were now diesels not steam and far more frequent.

This was a huge blow as it meant we no longer had a regular milk cheque which had formed the basis of our livelihood. However, our landlord offered us more arable land and we decided to move into pig breeding. The result was reasonable, but the market had a habit of fluctuating noticeably from time to time which resulted in considerable loss of income some years.
All farmers rely on the weather to sow and harvest crops and of course it was always unpredictable. We grew mainly sugar beet and barley and quickly learned which fields would be too wet in autumn to use a heavy sugar beet harvester. This year we had grown 80 acres of hay which proved to be a very rewarding crop as we had an extremely hot summer.

I had always wanted to marry a farmer ever since I had been on many enjoyable farming trips with school during the War years. I craved an outdoor life. I had looked forward to turning hay with a hay fork and stooking sheaves by hand – but we never did! Soon after the Second World War farm machinery became the order of the day, with hay turners and combine harvesters leading the way. It seemed all we had to do was lift heavy, square bales of hay and straw and stack them in the field in 6's and 8's ready to be picked up by a fork lift mounted on a tractor. Then they were carted to the stack yard and unloaded by hand on to an elevator (this was often my job). The person on the stack handled them yet again as he placed them into position. So each bale was actually handled 4 -6 times and I often wondered if mechanisation really did make things any easier? Now I know why we all suffer with bad backs in our old age and why we were distraught about the stack fire which had destroyed all our hard work.

We all loved the open-air life and wouldn't have changed it for any other job. My personal contribution was to produce eggs for the family and for sale. The latter had to be cleaned, weighed and graded. A lot went into the making of cakes for the W.I. Market every week. My other enterprise was rearing orphan lambs for our freezer and those of several friends. I bottle fed them four-hourly at first and then six-hourly which meant I didn't get much sleep. It was a cold and lonely job in the middle of the night when the rest of the family were tucked up in bed.

We held our annual Scout Camp in the spring again, this time at Brownsea Island in Poole Harbour, Dorset. This was where Baden-Powell had held his first ever Scout Camp in 1907. We took our own canoes but hired a sailing dinghy. Our food shopping was done in Poole and delivered to the island by boat. The only vehicle on the island was a small truck owned by the warden, who would normally meet campers at the landing stage and transport equipment to their site. But we had been badly delayed by traffic en route and were late arriving – after 5pm, so our ferryman put the canoes overboard one by one, assuring us that they would be on our bit of beach before we arrived – and they were! When we disembarked everyone had to carry their own kit, and a trek cart was provided for tents and other equipment. It was quite a long way uphill and down again to the beach before we could set up camp.

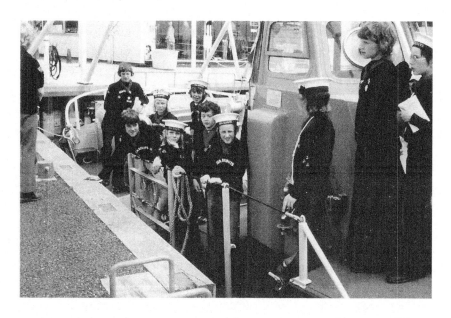

Visiting the first self-righting Lifeboat at Poole 1976

It was a very hot week and we were plagued with midges. Apparently, this was a regular occurrence so the warden provided us with special vapour lamps which helped to keep the midges at bay. We spent most of the week on or in the water but also explored the island and its wildlife. There was a nature reserve with hides to observe the birds on the mudflats, and I remember golden pheasants and red squirrels in the woodland but also a huge variety of seabirds nesting on the cliffs. Several Scouts earned their Naturalist Badge that week.

In July 1976 I helped organise the 'Sherwood 76' International Camp on Newark Showground. 1st Farndon entertained Scouts from the Faeroe Islands. They were lovely lads and we all got on very well. I wished we could have accepted their invitation of a reciprocal visit.

The hot weather continued until September and we finished harvest in record time. Our own holiday was delayed as we invited my cousin's son Darren to the farm for a week. When he had gone home, we packed our bags and set off for a campsite at Mevagissey in Cornwall, where Peter had just spent two scorching hot weeks. The day we travelled was reasonable, but the next day was very windy with a Force 9 gale spoiling a visit to Newquay. Then came the rain! Our well-used tent sagged with the weight of water and we had to bucket it out of the sleeping compartment. My canoe lay unused as huge waves lashed the shore. "When are you using that?" asked passers-by.

Dick had never visited Cornwall, so I drove him round to the prettiest bays saying, "Well it is nice here when the sun shines." I took him to Marazion and we walked across the causeway to visit St. Michael's Mount (interesting but wet!). When we returned to the car there appeared to be a problem. "Never mind," I said "there's always an AA man at Land's End." So we drove there only to find he was not a mechanic but only selling membership, which we already had. It appeared the alternator wasn't working so we were advised to drive back to camp avoiding the main roads. Next morning, we rang the local garage and a mechanic came out. Again, it was raining 'stair-rods' and work on it was impossible without cover, so he towed us to the garage and the problem was put right. The charge was £30! However, this was in the days before bank cards, credit cards or any form of bank ID - only a cheque book. The garage owner insisted on 'phoning our bank to ensure we had £30 in the account! How times have changed!

One morning the rain stopped and the sun came out for about half an hour. We went down to the nearest cove and sat on a wall and chatted to another couple. "I knew we should have gone to Bognor as usual," I said. The woman replied: "We've just come from there and it's no better." Every morning we vowed to go home the next day if there was no improvement, but we stuck it out. It was a long time before we visited Cornwall again and I never persuaded Dick to camp in this country again.

October found us back at Holme Pierrepont for the National Sea Scout Regatta, and at half-term camping at Longridge on the River Thames near Marlow, which is the Headquarters of Sea Scouting. The year ended with my brother Harry and his wife Jean's Silver Wedding in December.

Chapter 15

DENMARK & LOTS OF SCOUTING (1977-1979)

On March 22nd 1977 David joined the Royal Navy at HMS Raleigh, a shore-based training establishment near Plymouth. We saw him off at Newark Station and then we joined a party of local pig farmers for a five-day coach trip to Denmark. We stayed in a hotel at Odense on Funen Island - the middle one of them. Dick and I were allocated the Bridal Suite for some unknown reason, so we had inquisitive farmers knocking on our door to observe the large mural hanging above our bed. We had been married for over twenty years!

We visited numerous pig farms, abattoirs and canning factories. Everything was spotlessly clean wherever we went. Food, clothing and many other commodities were very expensive though. Some Danish youngsters spent Friday nights dancing in the disco on the ferry to England in order to buy their jeans much more cheaply, and then they would dance their way home again on the Saturday or Sunday night!

I always wished we could have had two more days in order to visit Copenhagen.

This was the Queen's Silver Jubilee year (1977) so there were lots of celebrations locally as well as in London. The Scouts took part in a Float Parade at Farndon depicting Scouting through the years.

In mid-May we were in Plymouth for David's Passing in Parade and then in July I returned for his Passing out Parade, taking my friend Madge with me as Dick was busy haymaking. David's 'Chief' invited me into his office to tell me how well he had done and that he had been recommended for the Specially Selected Seamanship Training Scheme. I felt very proud of him but I know how much he had benefitted from being a Sea Scout. He remained in the Royal Navy until 1981 and after leaving, pursued a career in carpentry and joinery within the boatbuilding industry. Boats and boating remain his lifelong passion. In that time, he had served aboard HMS Achilles on a Mediterranean deployment and completed a 16-week change-over from HMS Achilles to HMS Bacchante in Gibraltar. They exercised in the North Atlantic with visits to Norway, and other European visits including Belgium. Aboard HMS Bacchante he visited Bermuda and completed a lengthy tour with other NATO ships along the east coast of the USA and Canada, culminating in a goodwill visit to Iceland, the first visit by a Royal Navy ship since the 'Cod War'. I still have all the letters he wrote home to us and many souvenirs from different countries.

Our summer Scout Camp this year was in North Wales. We joined up with 1st Norwell Scouts so that we could afford a coach, and we hired a large van for equipment and, of course, I towed the canoe trailer! We had found a site on a farm on the promontory near the Portmeirion Italianate village. It was on the (Afon Dwyfyd) River Dwyfyd estuary where we sailed and canoed. When the tide was out, it left a large pool for swimming. We also took the canoes to Black Rock Sands for some canoe sea surfing, visited Portmadoc and took the Ffestiniog Railway up to the slate village. The two troops got on well together and it was an excellent camp.

After the annual regatta at Holme Pierrepont we took part in a two-day canoe slalom at Newark Lock and also had a few days camping at Drumhill in Derbyshire, where we did plenty of hill walking.

In November some of the troop took part in a four-night Gang Show at Newark Palace Theatre. It was a huge success!

In the spring of 1978 I visited Percy Thrower's garden, Magnolias, near Shrewsbury. It was somewhere I had always wanted to visit as I was a great fan of his. I was not disappointed; it was a really lovely garden and the magnolias were at their best. In June we had a party for Peter's 21st birthday at South Muskham Village Hall, as we didn't have a village hall in Rolleston until some years later.

The main Scouting event was the Summer Camp which we again shared with 1st Norwell Scouts. We had chosen the Lake District and camped on Church Stile Farm at Strands, a small village which is now known as Nether Wasdale. Getting there was a memorable nightmare for me. I was towing the canoe trailer carrying a dozen canoes on the M6 when a tyre blew on the trailer. I was being followed by another Scout Leader who quickly alerted me. The problem was there were ten miles of road works and the hard shoulder was being used as a lane, so there was nowhere to go, only a steep grass bank!

The Police soon spotted us and were very helpful, but I had to confess I didn't carry a spare trailer tyre or wheel (they are quite small). After un-hitching the trailer, I had to drive a long way to the nearest garage and then return the full ten miles of road works to retrieve it. When we finally arrived at the campsite it was about 6pm and it was pouring with rain and had been all day. The field was already like a quagmire, but the Scouts and other Leaders had pitched all the tents and got a meal cooking. Luckily most boys had brought wellies with them at my suggestion, though not normally part of a Scout's kit. We did a lot of canoeing on Wastwater and on the sea at St. Bees Head plus two days hill walking.

That week was memorable as we had a Scout with bad conjunctivitis needing a visit to the doctor and another Scout broke his elbow, requiring hospital treatment. 'It never rains but it pours!' On the last day we decided to canoe down the River Irt, the small river coming from the lower end of Wastwater. However, the recent rain meant the river was high and overhanging trees made progress hazardous. In the end I visualised taking home some headless

Scouts so we abandoned the trip. I seem to recall that when we were leaving home to go to camp, parents would say, "We hope you have good weather." I used to tell them the weather was the least of my worries, I just hoped to bring them all home in one piece! It was always quite a responsibility. I must remind you that in those days almost every Scout carried a sheath knife on his belt and a pen-knife in his pocket. They were used properly and sensibly and I do not recall in twenty years of Scouting there ever having been an incident involving a knife of any kind.

In the autumn David's ship HMS Bacchante was in Liverpool and they had an open day for families. I drove to Liverpool alone and found him in good spirits. He introduced me to his shipmates and showed me their living quarters. There were twenty-four of them in a very small mess and I was amazed at how clean and tidy it was. They told me they were only allowed three of each item of clothing, one being worn, one to wear and one at the laundry (dhobi). This also included smaller items as well. Perhaps I should have enforced this rule at home?

In December we had severe flooding at Fiskerton and on Kelham Road, and in the New Year, heavy snow and very icy conditions. Travelling was affected throughout the country with many roads impassable. David had weekend leave planned, but because of the severe weather decided a safer bet was to spend the weekend at one of his shipmate's parents' pub just outside Exeter. They got snowed in and he and his mates missed the ship sailing from Plymouth. They weren't the only ones! They all had to catch the train to Rosyth and wait for Bacchante to arrive. They then sailed to Stavanger in Norway.

Edward began his two years' work experience prior to going to Brackenhurst Agricultural College at Southwell. He was working on Mr Cressy's farm which was nearly a mile from the road to Oxton. On Christmas morning I had to take him to work in very deep snow. There was a small car blocking our way at Fiskerton. Four men stopped to help and picked it up and literally threw it onto the grass verge – it almost landed in the ditch. The road was treacherous all the way to the farm lane. I could see it was impassable so Edward had to walk the rest of the way. As he disappeared into the snow drifts I remember wondering if I should ever see him again. It was still dark with a clear sky and one solitary star. I decided it must have been the 'Star of Bethlehem'. Edward didn't get home for two nights and then had to use the biggest tractor to get home.

This was the start of 1979 and there was more heavy snow in February. I remember two hundred motorists were stranded in Cumbria. This was again followed by more floods.

One of the reps, who visited the farm regularly, invited us to camp in his field at Barlow in Derbyshire. So at Spring Bank Holiday we took the Patrol Leaders from both troops for a long weekend. It rained almost all the time which curtailed our activities and waterlogged the site. But we made the best of it.

My main memory is of us cooking Sunday lunch in our usual way, roast beef cooked in a clay oven in the ground with a chimney. One of the Scouts boiled a lettuce thinking it was a cabbage but otherwise all went well and the beef was excellent. We asked our friend's four-year-old grandson, who had spent some time in the muddy field with us, if he would like to join us for Sunday lunch. He was delighted and sat cross-legged on a piece of wood. When his plate was full of meat and vegetables he asked, "Is there any horseradish sauce?" I'm afraid we had to disappoint the little culinary four-year-old, but made a mental note in case we had guests in the future. When we left, we had to apologise profoundly for the bad state of the field but there was nothing we could do about it, only return the following weekend with a suitable thank-you gift.

In May we celebrated Edward's 18th birthday and after gaining his certificate at college he came home to work on the farm.

In June David came home on leave for three weeks and suggested we had a trip to Scotland's west coast, as he had visited some beautiful places whilst on Fishery Protection, Ullapool in particular. We set off in our bright Daytona Yellow Cortina, taking his friend Bob from Rolleston, with us. David was learning to drive so he took the wheel a lot of the time. We drove up the length of Loch Lomond and then across to Glencoe and Fort William. While here we drove into Glen Nevis so that I could re-call my climb of the Ben in 1950. How I wished I could do it again! We continued north as our plan was to visit the Isle of Skye. First, we took a boat trip on Loch Alsh to see the seals and visit Eilean Donan Castle. We stayed in a nearby hotel that night and crossed the Kyle of Lochalsh to Skye the next morning. We did a thorough tour of the island visiting Dunvegan Castle and enjoying a close-up view of the Cuillin Mountains, so often only seen from afar. We spent the night in Portree and explored the town before re-tracing our steps and discovering Glen Brittle, which we just had to explore. It was a beautiful spot, and David and I would have loved to have camped in the small tent we had brought with us. Bob wasn't so keen, so we pressed on to Kyleakin for the night. After dinner I remember walking on a rocky beach in the late evening in broad daylight (about 11pm) and David saying, "I could live here and build boats." Next day we drove to Ullapool where the idea of the holiday was mooted, explored the town and watched fishermen prepare their boats for a night at sea.

We stayed in a bed & breakfast overnight before starting our long drive home. We broke the journey at a house near Fort William. The landlady asked if one of us was musical as she had spotted David's guitar. Bob and David said they both were, so she then said, "I have a piano which hasn't been played since my daughter left home to get married. I'd be delighted to hear one of you play it." So in the evening Bob obliged and the landlady, other guests, David and I sat and listened. Bob played for about 45 minutes without any music and when he got up from the piano, the landlady said, "I don't know how you remember it all." Bob replied, "I just made it up as I went along." Hats off to Bob, he still is a brilliant pianist! Next day was a quick dash home, as we had to be back for my niece Jill's 21st birthday party the following evening. We had done 1,361 miles in the week.

Soon afterwards I was offered a part-time job with a company doing market research with farmers. I was given a deadline for each assignment and arranged my own time-table. It was not until the foot and mouth outbreak in 2000, and farm visits were curtailed, that I decided to quit. It had been an enjoyable experience for over twenty years.

Scout Camp that summer was in Eskdale in North Yorkshire in the village of Sleights. We camped in a farmer's field with the River Esk just across the road. We enjoyed lots of canoeing and some Scouts accompanied me paddling canoes downstream to Whitby. We found it extremely difficult paddling back upstream as the tide was going out. So the next time we went, we got one of the Leaders to take the canoe trailer to Whitby and we rode back in the minibus. We also visited Robin Hood's Bay and canoe surfed at Sandsend. One evening when we were exploring a hillside behind the camp, we heard a loud crash and saw a huge branch drop from an oak tree near to the gate to our field. Some of it fell on the road and the Scouts left in camp were quick to act. They stopped the traffic and two of them ran to the farm to report it. They returned with a selection of saws and axes. We returned from the hillside walk in great haste. Most of the branch fell in the field where we had often parked our cars but luckily not that day. The debris on the road was cut up and carried into the field and a number of the scouts earned their Axemanship Badge that evening. The two ladies who owned the farm were very appreciative of their quick thinking and hard work and rewarded them with a tray of eggs - it was a chicken farm!

Soon after our return from Summer Camp some of us were involved in the big International Camp at Walesby. As we had a minibus, I was asked to pick up some Lebanese Scouts from Nottingham Railway Station late in the evening. There were about ten of them and they had very little kit with them – no tent, no sleeping bag, no food, just pretty well what they stood up in. They said they slept "under the stars" at home. We fed them and found them camping gear. Luckily the weather was very hot, which suited them.

Back home in September 1979 Edward began his agricultural course at Brackenhurst College in Southwell, and there was news that David was going on deployment to the USA and his first port of call was to be Bermuda.
At the end of November, we put on another Gang Show at Newark Palace Theatre. Again, it was very popular and a great success.

Chapter 16

NARROW BOATS, ART CLASS & RHS (1980-1982)

1980 brought more snow and ice at the beginning of the year and sadly we sold the last of the pigs. From then on, we reared beef cattle and still grew some arable crops. David learnt to drive, bought his first car, an MG1300, and went to Chatham to join the Reserve Ship Squadron. I took Auntie Vera to Brighton to see a garden show put on by her brother-in-law. She stayed with Auntie Freddie while I stayed with my school friend Barbara. At Easter we spent a weekend with Dick's brother Norman and his wife Beryl at Kidlington near Oxford. We visited Woodstock and found Churchill's grave at Bladon. We visited the University Gardens which were very colourful with lots of spring flowers, but it was bitterly cold.

In May I began my part-time job at Fiskerton Wharf where Mr Radford had a small fleet of five Hoseasons narrow boats for hire. They went out on Fridays and Saturdays from May to October, and my job was as receptionist, demonstrator and replenishing bed linen etc. I did this job for six years. Also in May we celebrated our Silver Wedding with a party at the farm and we bought ourselves an Austin Allegro.

Our Scout Camp that summer was on Northey Island in the Blackwater Estuary near Maldon in Essex. We were quite isolated but there was a lot of wildlife which we all enjoyed. We had to go back across the causeway to canoe and sail at Maldon. One day while we were canoeing David made a surprise visit from Chatham. He stood on the causeway beside his car trying to attract our attention. I paddled over and told him to "carry on to camp and put the kettle on – we'll be back soon." We returned to the camp to a welcome cup of tea. After camp we spent two nights at Baden-Powell House in London and visited the Maritime Museum at Greenwich, the Cutty Sark and the Gypsy Moth IV, in which Sir Francis Chichester had been the first person to circumnavigate the world taking 226 days in 1966-1967. Before returning home, we spent an afternoon at Gilwell Park which is the headquarters of Scouting with acres of camping space and every conceivable activity loved by Scouts.

My cousin Joan and husband Clifford decided on a narrow boat holiday but had no experience whatsoever, so I took them upstream to Gunthorpe and let them carry on without me until next morning, when I re-joined them at Barrow-on-Soar. We got as far as Lime Kiln Lock in Leicester that week before turning for home – 24 locks in all.

In October I met Barbara in the Cotswolds and we spent a few days at a lovely hotel in Chalford. We visited the village of Slad, home to the author Laurie Lee of 'Cider with Rosie' fame. We had lunch at the pub he frequented. That night we went to a concert in Stroud. Next day we headed for the small town of Tetbury with nice shops and coffee houses. Of course we sampled them before continuing to Westonbirt Arboretum, where we had been assured the colours would be at their best. Well, they were spectacular. The first Acer (maple) I spotted was such a bright red it was hard to believe it was a living tree. There were hundreds of them in all shades of red, orange, yellow, green and variegated in all shapes and sizes. One morning we noticed Burleigh Court Hotel was open for coffee. So in we went, only to find that the owner's mother was a friend of mine in Nottingham. After entertaining us with coffee and cakes he showed us round his lovely hotel. I stayed there the following year – more about that later. We walked on Minchinhampton Common which is clothed in wild flowers, including orchids in spring, then we drove through the Golden Valley where the trees really did form a canopy of gold.

All our hard work in raising money for a village hall in Rolleston came to fruition in November when we held the opening ceremony and the first dance of many. In December David left the Royal Navy and was home in time to celebrate his 21st Birthday.

In 1981 I added more interest to my already busy life. January found me joining an art class run by Marjorie Arnfield in Southwell. I had been hopeless at art in school, but was inspired by my friend Barbara's father, who was an amateur artist. I had watched him painting on numerous occasions and just wished I could too. Here was an opportunity to try oil paints for a short spell and then watercolours. I enjoyed it so much that I stayed with Marjorie's class and painted with them, mostly in oils, for the next fifteen years. I found it very relaxing and rewarding and during that time painted dozens of pictures. Many I gave as presents or to charity. There were a few commissions and the rest hang around the house or are put away in boxes.

Marjorie organised many painting trips abroad, mostly to France and Greece, but as we were still busy on the farm I was unable to take part. I did however, have two long weekends in France with the class. The first was to Paris where we visited several art galleries and had a trip out to Barbizon and Fontainebleau. We had time to do some sketching, we ate in a restaurant on the Left Bank of the Seine on the Saturday evening (that spelt 'Paris' for me). We also had a trip on the Seine on a Bateau Rouge and visited Notre Dame, the Sacré-Cœur and the Pompidou Centre among other famous sights.

On our second visit in 1982 we stayed in Evreux from where we visited Monet's Garden at Giverny, and saw his famous bridge and water lily paintings in Paris. More galleries were on the itinerary and we visited Rouen on our way home. These visits and the interesting people I met fired my enthusiasm for art – a subject I had previously had little interest in.
The second new interest this year was a horticultural evening class covering two winters, which culminated in the gaining of the RHS Certificate.

The narrow boat season started at Easter and David (who had worked for Mr Radford on the boats, prior to joining the Royal Navy) again worked at the weekends on the boats while he attended his carpentry and joinery course at Kirkby-in-Ashfield. He joined Fiskerton Wharf as a Trainee Manager after completion of his course in the summer.

Dick and I made our first visit to Normandy together in June for the re-union of the 11th Armoured Division. We stayed with Madame Groult. Her late husband had been a local judge and she lived in a lovely big house in the hamlet of Montamy. She spoke no English so we had to manage with my school-girl French which was pretty reasonable but by no means fluent! It soon improved! Over that weekend we were shown around the local area, and on the Sunday a service was held at the memorial to the 11th Armoured Division just outside the town of Flers, followed by a banquet at a hotel in the village of Le Beny Bocage.

Next day we set off for our second week camping in south Brittany (having already had a week in north Brittany.)

When we returned home it was almost time for Scout Camp which we held in the grounds of Ford Castle in Northumberland. From here we visited Lindisfarne, crossing the causeway at low tide and had a boat ride out to the Farne Islands. We also did a lot of canoeing.

We celebrated the wedding of Prince Charles and Lady Diana Spencer while there, with a scrumptious alfresco meal followed by fireworks. Some of us had accepted an invitation to watch the wedding on TV at the local school house.

The year ended with a heavy snowfall on December 14th which lay 8" (200mm) deep until New Year's Eve.

1982 began very cold and wet. There were floods at Fiskerton and on 11th January the temperature was -27°C, on the 13th -21°C, and on the 14th -15°C.

I received a letter from my mother's cousin Leolin, in California, inviting me to join her on an eighteen-day holiday in Switzerland in August with a party of Americans, to look at the alpine flowers. How could I say no! There was one other English woman (with her Canadian cousin) on the trip, named Rosalind, with whom I became friendly and who, nearly forty years later, I still visit at her home in the New Forest.

On April 2nd Argentine troops invaded the Falkland Islands and so began the Falklands War. We were thankful David had left the Royal Navy although he was still in the Reserves. Many of his shipmates went to serve in the South Atlantic and survived but Britain suffered many casualties and 255 dead. On June 14th 1982 Argentina surrendered.

That spring was quite busy. I visited Cambridge with the art class and spent a week with Barbara at Worthing, having dropped my aunt off at Hove to stay with her sister. Then Dick's niece Sally brought her son Alex to stay on the farm for a few days, and Edward had a big party for his 21st Birthday in May. At the end of the month, we all went off to Surrey (girlfriends included) to cousin Nicky Nimmy's 21st birthday party at the Cricketers Hotel near Ascot. While in the area we visited the famous Savill Gardens.

In June we had very heavy rain and more flooding in our area and the River Trent was ten feet above normal. We had some excellent vegetables in the garden, sixteen varieties all at once!

On July 19th the great day was here for the arrival of our visitor from California. I met her at Heathrow and we spent a night in the area in order to visit Kew Gardens and the RHS Gardens at Wisley. Leolin had been a Professor of Botany at the University of California at Berkeley, where she lived. She had written a book about the flora of Mount Diablo. She asked to visit the Herbarium at Kew in order to find her book. We waited ages before we were allowed in as we didn't have an appointment. Then we couldn't find the book! There were some red faces all around!

After a few days at home on the farm Dick joined us for a short break in Cornwall, as Leolin had never been there in her younger days while living in England (she was now 74 years old). En route we spent a night in the hotel I had discovered in the Cotswolds, where the proprietor's wife took us to see wild orchids growing on Minchinhampton Common. This was an excellent start to our trip and Leolin was absolutely delighted.

We drove south to Cornwall and found a hotel near to the Lizard and Land's End peninsular, where for the next few days our visitor photographed hundreds of wild flowers, in addition to visiting a number of picturesque coastal villages. We had lunch with her mother's friend at Exmouth and visited my Scout Troop who were camping in the area. Then we drove along the south coast to Sussex, where Leolin spent a few days with her cousin Freddie at Hove, and I visited my school friend Barbara at Worthing. On our return home I took her to stay with another cousin in Nottingham (my Auntie Vera) where other members of the family called to see her.

Chapter 17

HOLIDAY OF A LIFETIME (1982)

By the middle of August, it was time for the two of us to fly off to Switzerland and join the group of Americans with whom we were to spend the next eighteen days. We covered most of Switzerland looking at lots of alpine flowers and enjoying the wonderful hospitality of nine different five-star hotels. It really was my 'holiday of a lifetime' and all paid for! We flew into Geneva and stayed for two nights in a hotel overlooking the railway station. This suited me as I had always had a fascination for trains of different types.

The Swiss ones were long, sleek, quiet and always ran on time. The station was very busy and held my interest while Leolin rested. Later we toured the city and visited the gardens, where we saw chipmunks and myrtle trees in blossom. Next day the coach took us up the Souleve Mountain where we saw lots of wild flowers and on to Monettier, where Sunday lunch was served in a lovely hillside restaurant with musicians playing stringed instruments.

Next day we were taken to Les Diablerets – a small mountain village and ski resort. There were masses of alpine flowers on the steep slopes and a fast-flowing river through the village. Our coach trip next morning was up over the Col des Mosses, a high mountain pas which is closed for much of the year. We visited Château d'Oex and had lunch in Gstaad (a famous haunt of film stars). In the afternoon our driver braved fourteen zig-zags of steep mountain road to an alpine garden at Champex. It was very colourful and well worth the journey.

After a second night in Les Diablerets we set out for what I think was my favourite stopover. First, we drove through the Rhone Valley up the St. Bernard Pass to visit the mountain rescue dogs, with hillsides covered in grapevines all the way to Visp where we turned off onto the only road up to Zermatt. At Tasch we boarded the local train into Zermatt and then transferred to horse-drawn carriages with our luggage on the roof and continued on to the Hotel Mont Cervin – owned by the well-known Zeiler family. This was the 'crème de la crème'. Our room was at the back of the hotel, but that didn't matter as when we woke next morning there was the Matterhorn with the sun rising behind it. I could photograph it without getting out of bed and did so for the next half hour with the changing light.

It was a beautiful day and everything went according to plan. We took the train on the rack and pinion railway up the Gornergrat (313mtrs) from where the view of the Matterhorn was at its best. We spent the afternoon walking back down the mountain to Zermatt, first having a picnic lunch in the warm sunshine. We saw and photographed dozens of different species of wild flowers, some in crevices or under overhanging rocks, others emerging from the snow. Patterns in the snow made by the wind made the scenery even more picturesque. Lower down the mountain there were a number of cows with the famous cowbells round their necks jangling away. We saw the red rescue helicopter fly over towards the Matterhorn to pick up another unlucky climber. Our driver said that was number 17 that year. In due course I painted two pictures of the Matterhorn and took 72 photos that day. It had been a most memorable day. After a superb dinner that evening, we danced for a while before spending our second night in this beautiful hotel.

In the morning we left the Rhone Valley at Brig and turned south, over the picturesque Simplon Pass, into Italy to our next stop at Locarno, situated on the northern tip of Lake Maggiore. We arrived at another very smart resort and the lovely Hotel Muralto for us to enjoy for two nights. We spent the next morning on the lake and visiting Brissago Island where we saw some exotic flowers, including Gerberas which were the first I had seen and I fell in love with them - I have grown them many times since. Our journey then took us back into Switzerland to the Engerdine Region – a fertile valley of farmsteads, one of which was the home of our driver's girlfriend. The family were expecting us for coffee (or wine!) and were our hosts that day. They took us up the steep hillside standing in hay carts - sort of wire cages on wheels pulled by a tractor. It was a hairy ride! At the midway point there were buildings where the cows were housed and milked for 2 – 3 months on their way up and down the mountain. The harsh weather conditions only allowed them to stay on the mountain plateau for 3 months in summer, where we were taken to see them milked in a milking bale – a small portable milking unit. From these the milk was carried down to the farmhouse in a large pipeline. In the worst of the winter weather all the animals lived underneath the farmhouse, providing them with a certain amount of warmth and in return they helped to warm the house.

The next area to explore was the Swiss National Park where we stayed in the village of Tschiev. There I saw my first edelweiss, masses of them, growing on a grassy hillside. A walk in the Park revealed lots of small wild animals such as marmots and chipmunks.

Next, we had a long drive up the Fluela Pass with lots of snow, via Davos and Klosters, to a one-night stop at Chur. Here the hotel proprietor showed us his wonderful collection of horse-drawn carriages. The next outing took us through another snow-covered pass – the Susten Pass - to the picturesque Gletcher Gorge where we ventured onto a board walk only feet from a raging torrent. It was quite scary! We stopped for a while in Brienz to visit a magnificent shop selling hand-made wooden articles, where we bought souvenirs. Then we travelled via Interlaken to Grindelwald for one of the highlights of our holiday. We stayed in another first-class hotel where my friend Rosalind and her cousin were given the Presidential Suite. The next day we took the rack and pinion train via Kleine Scheideg up the Eiger Mountain. Twice we stopped to get out into a concrete building to look at the view. One of these viewing platforms appeared in one of the James Bond films. At the top of the mountain we walked in the Ice Palace and had lunch in the restaurant, and later took a lift to the summit where we walked out onto another viewing platform. It was extremely cold and a heavy blizzard meant there was a complete 'whiteout'. We couldn't see a thing!

After our departure from Grindlewald we paid a brief sightseeing visit to Bern – administrative capital of Switzerland – a smart city with lovely shops. One night was spent in Basel, an historical city, and we were on our way to our final two-night stay in Lucerne – another beautiful resort beside the lake. Unfortunately, it rained heavily for our boat ride and we were unable to visit Mt. Pilatus but the shops were nice. We flew home from Zurich the next day after a wonderful eighteen-day holiday, staying in nine different top-class hotels. It had definitely been my holiday of a lifetime.

At Heathrow Pete and Denise met me, while Leolin and most of the others flew back to the USA.

Late summer 1982, fabulous holiday over, I picked up my part-time jobs again – narrow boats at Fiskerton, farm surveys for the market research company and baking cakes for the W.I Market. Then there was a garden full of fruit to be made into jam, and vegetables to preserve for winter.
For most of December the farmhouse was in chaos, as we had central heating installed and a lovely Austrian Tirolia cooking range, which proved a real treasure. Right up until Christmas Day we had teething problems with the heating and had to call out the plumber. But in the end it was a real asset and we wondered how we had managed so long without it.

Chapter 18

JUST A NORMAL YEAR (1983)

At the beginning of 1983 Peter and Denise got engaged and celebrated with an evening meal at the Haven near Bottesford and a party in Rolleston Village Hall. We had a lot of snow in February but I managed to get around doing farm surveys and went back to my art class. I also joined an evening German class, because I was planning to take some Scouts to camp at Emmendingen in the Black Forest with whom Newark was about to be twinned.

We were privileged to have a visit from the Chief Scout at a venue in Nottingham.

In May my friend Rosalind, who I had met on the Swiss holiday, came to stay and I took her to Derbyshire for a few days, where we visited Chatsworth and some of the annual Well Dressings.

July heralded Scout Camp once more – back in Eskdale in North Yorkshire, near the village of Sleights on a chicken farm owned by two lady farmers. There was just a country lane between our field and the River Esk. Here we had lots of fun in our canoes. Our favourite game was to tie balloons onto the stern of our canoe and paddle round, trying to burst everyone else's whilst preserving our own. There was lots of capsizing (sometimes deliberately), but it was a shallow river and of course we always wore lifejackets in any kind of boat. It was also safe to swim there. Some of the older boys went off in threes to hike on the moors carrying a small tent and the necessary equipment and food for an overnight camp. This activity earned them a prestigious badge. We visited Whitby twice, some of us paddling downstream in our canoes, but again had difficulty getting back, as the tide went out. On the second occasion someone brought the canoe trailer for the return journey and we walked back to camp. We also visited Robin Hood's Bay and did some canoe surfing at Sandsend.

When the harvest was in and we had celebrated with our usual wonderful Rolleston Harvest Festival and supper, I went off to stay with my school friend Barbara at Worthing. She took me to see lovely gardens including Leonardslea, which was new to me and was very colourful as it was now October. I visited other friends and family while in the area. One evening we dined at a smart hotel and for the first time ever indulged in a Châteaubriand – a small, extremely tender joint of beef which is carved at the table and usually shared. It was delicious and to this day remains one of my favourite special treats. I returned home, but three weeks later was back in Worthing for Barbara's marriage to Reg – she had lost her previous husband Don three and a half years previously.

The year ended with me cooking dinner for the whole family on New Year's Eve.

Chapter 19

NEW FRIENDS – FRENCH & GERMAN (1984)

In 1984 Newark's idea of twinning with Emmendingen in Germany's Black Forest came to fruition. In April a contingency of Germans came to Newark for the inaugural ceremony. As a committee member I was asked to host a headmaster and his wife, Herr Mossner and Sylvia. He was about Dick's age and had been a Luftwaffe Pilot during World War 2. They didn't speak English so we survived on my small amount of German that I had learnt at evening class. He broke the ice by suggesting that our Spitfires were better than their Messchersmitts, as he had been shot down twice in them.

The main ceremony took place in the Newark Castle grounds where gifts were exchanged by the Mayors of Emmendingen and Newark. This was followed by a performance from the Sealed Knot re-enactment group. There was a visit to the English Civil War Monument at Queen's Sconce in Newark. We then went for an excellent lunch at Kelham Hall and took them on coach outings to Sherwood Forest and Belvoir Castle.

Later in the month there was a visit from the Queen to Southwell Minster to distribute Maundy Money. I managed to catch a glimpse of her as she passed through Averham.

Towards the end of April, I went with my art teacher Marjorie Arnfield and some of my art class members to Higham Hall in the Lake District, where we received tuition on painting and sketching some of the beautiful Lakeland scenery.

We were very busy with the narrow boats during May but I had time off at the end of the month. On the 26th May Peter and Denise were married at Bleasby Church, followed by a reception at the Saracen's Head Hotel in Southwell.

Three days later Dick and I set off for France for another 11th Armoured Division re-union. We spent the first night on an excellent campsite at Thury-Harcourt beside the River Orne. The next evening we were to meet up in the village of Le Beny-Bocage from where we were led to the home of our hosts, Jean and Monique Cahagnes, where Jean's 50th birthday party was in full swing. We arrived about 9pm and went to bed about 2am, having waded through umpteen courses of food and wine to match. The next morning my head was thumping. "Would you like a boiled egg?" asked Monique, thinking perhaps their continental breakfast wouldn't suffice. "No thank you," I didn't really feel like eating anything at all!

We were soon off to our first engagement and parade at Pont du Taureau, a small bridge named after the emblem of the 11th Armoured Division. Down this narrow lane and across this little bridge the whole Division had marched and driven, because the main road had been blocked by Germans.

This little bridge was the route they took to liberate the town of Flers, which became the centrepiece of our many visits over the next twenty-plus years, and where the memorial had been built a couple of miles outside the town.

On Sunday morning a service was held there with General 'Pip' Roberts and his wife present, he was the Division's General and the youngest General in the army on D-Day (he was only 38).

This was followed by lunch in a huge marquee on the fairground. Later the veterans marched through the town to the chateau. Most people departed for home on the Monday, but we had planned to go camping in the Loire Valley. However, Jean and Monique persuaded us to stay on with them for a few days. They showed us their village and a vast collection of American Army vehicles parked in the square for the weekend. They took us to Caen and Bayeux and to the Divisions Museum at St. Martin des Besaces, to which at a later date we donated the original Regimental Diary (we have a copy).

We visited numerous cemeteries near the sites of battles and found graves of many of Dick's comrades. We did this on subsequent visits until we had found them all. I did sometimes ask myself if I really wanted to spend part of my summer holiday traipsing round Normandy's cemeteries. But I concluded that, yes, it was important to Dick that he knew where his comrades had fallen, and I supported him in his quest, which took some time before we eventually found the one that had eluded him. I think for Dick it was a sense of closure that he had finally been able to pay his last respects to them all. We had been in Cahagnes a full week before we left for our camping holiday.

After a night at Château Gontier we headed for the coast stopping briefly at Jard-sur-Mer, but preferred Châtelaillon Plage for the night's stop. We spent the next day in La Rochelle which we loved – the patisserie shops were worth a photograph. We drove back inland to Argentan Château before finding a lovely site at Montreuil Bellay. Here we stayed for seven very hot days and nights visiting as many chateaux along the Loire as we could manage in the heat. These included Chillon, Azay-le-Rideau, Ussé, Saumur, Langeais, and the troglodyte caves at Dampiere-sur-Loire. We should have returned home a week earlier, but the weather in England was very wet so the hay was not ready. We had left Peter and his cousin Tony in charge and we phoned them each evening for an update on the weather.

When we did get home it was all hands on deck in the hayfield and lots of soft fruit to pick and turn into jam.

Dick celebrated his 65th Birthday that July so we hired two narrow boats from Fiskerton for a trip down to Farndon and back for the family and lots of friends. This was followed by an evening barbeque.

Another celebration this year was the marriage of my nephew Nigel to Sue at West Bridgford.

In October Dick and I availed ourselves of two spare seats on a coach taking Newark Operatic Society to sing in Emmendingen. I wanted to find a campsite for a party of Newark Scouts the following summer, so we stayed with Herr Mossner and his family and he showed us round the Schillingerberg area. We were introduced to Farmer Haas up in the hills who offered us a large sloping field at the top of which was a pine forest. He pointed to a fence post split down the middle by lightening! It turned out to be an excellent site for us.

The year ended with an award ceremony when the County Commissioner bestowed on me the 15-year service ribbon for my time as a Sea Scout Leader. It was a proud moment. It had been a challenge but I had enjoyed it immensely with a great bunch of lads.

Chapter 20

BAD NEWS, THEN LOTS OF VISITORS (1985-1986)

1985 began quietly but became busier as the year progressed. My friend Madge stayed for a few days at New Year as usual but when she had departed it snowed heavily and the roads were extremely bad. It was also bitterly cold. The boys decided I was due for a new kitchen so they set to work and installed one. I was unable to get to my art and German classes but made use of my new knitting machine. By March the weather had improved so I was able to catch up with the market research farm surveys. Several Lincolnshire farmers had cade lambs (orphaned) to dispose of, so I bought some very cheaply and some were even given to me. All in all, I had about twenty to bottle feed every 4~6 hours which kept me rather busy. It's not much fun at 2am on a frosty morning when the little blighters won't suck and you keep thinking of the rest of the family tucked up in a warm bed! When they were reared, I sold some to my friends to keep their freezers stocked and we kept some for ourselves. One Sunday when David's girlfriend was having lunch with us, Eddie, always the joker, asked, "Is this Sooty or Sweep, Mum?" Jane put down her knife and fork and demanded of me, "This isn't one of yours Mrs Brettle, is it?" What could I say?

By now we were wondering whether we should give up the tenancy of the farm, both Peter and Edward had originally been told by the landlords they could follow their father's tenancy, provided they attended Agricultural College and gained the necessary qualifications. This they had both done, but the landlords changed their minds because building land was at a premium and they would sell some of our land for this purpose. There seemed little point in carrying on. After much deliberation and heartbreak we decided to give a year's notice to quit at Michaelmas 1986. We expected to remain in the house (hence the new kitchen) as had been the landlord's previous policy, but they reneged on this too. They were however compelled to find us accommodation.

Decisions finally made, the rest of 1985 was enjoyable. We had lots of visitors including members of the Mundingen Band from the Black Forest in Germany – a neighbouring town of our twin Emmendingen. In early May Dick and I spent a few days with his brother Norman and wife Beryl at the Little Uplands Country Club in Hampshire. We visited Meonstoke where the brothers had lived and had been to school at Exton, where they had sung in the church choir. We visited some old school friends living next door to their old house and many other favourite spots. We had lunch in the garden of The Shoe at Exton beside the River Meon where they had spent many happy hours as youngsters.

Later that month I went off to a county previously unexplored by me, Norfolk. I went there with my art class friends, Doris, Gwen, and Dorothy. We rented an apartment at Burnham Overy Staithe. Gwen knew the area and where we could find the best scenery for painting and sketching. It was a fabulous week.

In June we had a three week visit from an American lady I had befriended on the Swiss holiday in 1982. I met Eva at Heathrow Airport, and we stayed overnight with cousins Pat and Don at their house, Merry Tilers, visiting Windsor, the small Tussauds display at the station there and the Queen's Dolls House. Next morning we walked through the Azalea Bowl at the Savill Garden before returning home via Henley-on-Thames. We spent a week showing her the local area including Sherwood Forest and Charnwood Forest, and then we set off on a two-week tour of the Cotswolds, Devon and Cornwall. These were her chosen areas to visit.

We aimed for Chipping Camden and Broadway which she loved and we spent the night in a bed and breakfast near Bourton-on-the-Water, enjoying an evening meal at The Lamb Inn at Great Rissington. This proved to be an excellent choice and we have been there several times since, taking other friends with us. Bourton-on-the-Water was a real hit and so were the villages of Upper and Lower Slaughter. My visitor was obviously impressed with this beautiful part of our English countryside. We visited Burford and Bibury briefly and motored on down through Cirencester, Stroud and the Golden Valley, staying overnight at a small hotel at Amberley not far from the small town of Tetbury, near to Prince Charles' home. Next came the wonderful city of Bath and a whole day of sightseeing, before winding our way into Devon and our next stop at the Woody Bay Hotel, overlooking the sea near Porlock.

A cliff-top walk took us to the Huntsman's Inn for lunch the next day. Later we drove through the Valley of the Rocks to Lynton, Lynmouth, Porlock Weir and Bossington where we watched two men thatching a cottage roof. I later painted a picture from my photograph of them and one of the Pack-horse Bridge at Allerford. At the very pretty Selworthy Green we had a Devon cream tea on the lawn at a cottage. I remember Eva remarking how pretty the waitress was, saying, "They all have such lovely rosy cheeks – at home they are so unattractive." The quaint village of Clovelly really captured her heart so we walked down the steep cobbled hill and came back up in a Land Rover as it had started to rain.

After a night in another excellent hotel we drove down to Cornwall and visited Land's End and walked on the beach at Sennen Cove. The Lizard peninsular was covered in wild flowers, we would have liked to have spent more time there, but we had to press on as I knew of a bed and breakfast at Downderry, passing through Helston, Falmouth, Truro, Polperro and Looe en route. We were now heading along the south coast to Dorset and Hampshire but we were suddenly aware that something was amiss, the exhaust pipe was hanging off the car. We found a garage in Bridport but had to wait some time for it to be fixed. We went from café to café drinking tea and cold drinks as it was a very hot day. We finished up sitting on the pavement outside the garage in the searing heat. We had been in Bridport for four hours! Further on we found a bed and breakfast near Christchurch and then after a tour of the New Forest re-visited our lovely Clarehaven Hotel at Bognor.

The last leg of our tour took us into Surrey where our last night was spent at the Royal Foresters Hotel near Ascot. Next day I saw Eva on to an aeroplane at Heathrow for her flight back to the USA.

It had been a packed tour, but she was very happy with everything that she had seen of our beautiful English countryside and coastline. We kept in touch for about 10 years but then the letters stopped coming.

When I had got my breath back from Eva's visit it was time to set off for Scout Camp in the Black Forest in Germany. I had organised a twelve-day camp in the hills near Newark's twin town of Emmendingen, on a farm we had visited while over there with the Newark Operatic Society. We took a coach load of Scouts and Leaders from Newark District and were given a huge welcome by the local people. We camped with a large contingency of German Scouts from the Schillingerberg area and were given free access to lots of sporting activities such as swimming pools, football pitches and crazy golf etc. There was a tremendous reception at the Rathaus (town hall) where I made a short speech in German! Thank goodness for the evening classes.

We were also given a thorough sight-seeing tour of the town. On the last day the German Scouts organised a mock wedding where one of their girl Scouts married one of the boys. They had concocted all manner of costumes and there was singing and dancing. That evening we organised a huge campfire to which we invited other German Leaders, and several lots of parents, who brought us gifts of wine and beer and crates of soft drinks for the Scouts. I also received a large piece of smoked bacon to bring home.

Later in the summer some German Scouts came to camp at Walesby International Camp Site but someone else organised that.

In September our French friends, Jean and Monique came to stay at the farm. They were keen to see Robin Hood country and Nottingham as well as Southwell and Newark. We took them to Belvoir Castle and Lincoln where they were impressed with the Cathedral, but the highlight of the day for Jean was lunch at the Pie Shop on Steep Hill! A day in Derbyshire was spoilt by rain.

After their visit we had a break ourselves, staying with Dick's brother Norman and his wife Beryl at Kidlington. It had been a hectic year.

1986 was quieter as we began to wind down the farm, thinking we should be moving out in the autumn. But in fact there were complications in finding us suitable accommodation, so we stayed in the farmhouse for a further year.

Our last harvest 1986

We sold the livestock first and had a sale of machinery and effects later. The landlord found someone to farm the land for twelve months. All we did was to sit tight or take a holiday. We had officially retired.

We went off to spend Easter with Barbara and her husband Reg at Worthing, visiting Dick's niece Rosemary, her husband Pete and their family nearby and also my Auntie Freddie at Hove. In May David and some friends put a performance of 'Grease' on at the Palace Theatre at Newark, using mostly pupils from the Minster School in Southwell. It was a huge success with large audiences.

During the summer there were two outings with the art class - one to Suffolk to see the village of Dedham and the surrounding area, known for its paintings by Constable. The other was to the Royal Academy in London. In June I began a part-time job at Brinkley Nurseries with Celia Steven, daughter of the well-known Merryweather family of Bramley Apple fame. Here I was in my element propagating, pruning and potting plants by the hundred - just a taste of the career I would like to have followed.

We exchanged weekend visits with Norman and Beryl and these became more frequent now that we had retired from the farm.

In October I spent a week in Bath with three of my art friends, where Doris had a flat in a large house she owned on Lansdowne Crescent. We visited many beauty spots in the surrounding area to sketch and paint. We visited Laycock (where photography began), Castle Combe, Stourhead, Longleat and many more. We were also spoilt for choice with the lovely scenery in Bath. We found a different hostelry each evening for our main meal. On our way home we stopped at Westonbirt Arboretum to see the wonderful autumn colours of the Acers (Maples). We were not disappointed – it was tremendously spectacular.

So here we were, still in the farmhouse for yet another Christmas and the usual family get-together with aunts, uncles and cousins. We wished it could have continued thus.

I carried on with my art and German Classes and part-time jobs in order to generate some 'holiday money', as I was planning to give up Scouting and all the committees I was on, in order to spend a lot more time showing Dick some of the places he had never visited in Britain, and to return to Normandy in France where he had fought so bravely alongside his comrades after the D-Day landings.

Chapter 21

THE END OF AN ERA, BUT GOOD TIMES AHEAD (1987)

It was now 1987 and we waited with excitement for the arrival of our first grandchild. Luke Edward was born to Peter and Denise on May 9th (the 26th birthday of our youngest son Edward). There was a lot of celebrating to be done before we set off on our second visit to Jean and Monique at Cahagnes in France.

Jean and Monique usually had a surprise for us – this time it was to be the first Communion of Jean's God-daughter Nathanielle on the Sunday and we had been invited. We thought we had arrived in church plenty early enough but it was already packed. There were eleven other candidates with families. However, we were shown to VIP seats on the platform at the front and given French Service Sheets and Hymn Books and told we could take photos.

Stephane, the eldest son of Jean and Monique, had suggested I took my camera. It was a long but interesting and enjoyable service and we sang in French – even Dick! After some more photos outside we were taken to a restaurant in the next village where about thirty of us enjoyed a seven-course meal. We were told there would be eleven more such celebrations taking place in the vicinity and when, later in the afternoon replete with food and wine, we were taken to the local park and lake, there they all were, the girls in their white dresses and the boys in white suits – there was no mistaking them. We rowed on the lake, me in my best dress and high heels and Dick in his best suit, with Stephane doing his best to rock the boat and us protesting.

After a long walk and ice-creams all round (the French love to promenade), we went off to the family farm run by Monique's brother Daniel and his wife and their four children. I should mention that Stephane has an older sister, Laurence, who was training to be a nurse, and also a younger brother David, then still at school. About 7pm we returned to Cahagnes and were told to get spruced up because at 9pm we were to go back to the restaurant for another seven-course meal! We eventually crawled into bed at about 2am. Gosh! What a celebration it had been for one eleven-year-old girl's first Communion.

We had planned to go camping but we were persuaded to stay on at Cahagnes for another day or two. Stephane and his girlfriend Kristine took us to see the D-Day Museum at Arromanches and to La Pointe du Hoc, where the US Rangers had been decimated on D-Day while scaling the cliff face. This landmark remains as it was, with German guns and equipment left to rust, and camouflage netting torn to shreds, blowing in the wind. There were no birds singing and it smelt of death.

Next day Jean and Monique took us to Bayeux partly to see the famous tapestry, and on Wednesday we went to the market early with Jean to the small town of Villers Bocage. Dick happened to be wearing his Black Bull badge, emblem of the 11th Armoured Division. While at the cattle market one French farmer was convinced he was the bull salesman! Later that day we were taken to Flers to re-visit the chateau and the memorial to the 11th Armoured Division.

Monique loved cooking and entertaining and we always put on weight while there! At midday they had friends or relatives in for aperitifs lasting almost an hour. The visitors disappeared and then lunch was served for us and the family – usually five courses. Lettuce with a French dressing came as a separate course and so did the cheese – oh! the cheese - such a wonderful assortment. The ubiquitous French baguettes were always on the table, freshly baked and bought twice a day from the local boulangerie. This we could never resist and was responsible for our extra weight, I think! Wine often changed colour with different courses. Grandpa lived locally and always had lunch with us – with his cap on! He was over 90 years old and still kept a few animals of his own and grew a few vegetables. He brought a lettuce (called salade) every day at lunchtime.

By the Thursday they reluctantly let us go off camping. We drove to La Baule but it was extremely busy, so we had a look at the attractive little coastal town of Pornic and found a small campsite nearby. Next day we found a lovely campsite at La Boutinardiere with good facilities and right next to a beautiful sandy cove. We camped here for ten days touring the area and spending a lot of time in the sea as it was very hot. One day we drove over the bridge to the island of Noirmoutier which was quaint with lots of brightly coloured fishing boats. When we returned to England we stayed at Southsea for a night and spent a morning in Bosham, a favourite spot of ours, before driving home.

Back at the farm our new baby grandson Luke stayed with us overnight now and again. I was in my element. His Christening was held at St. Giles Church at Balderton on a very wet August Sunday. The party which followed at Thoroton included a hog roast, so everywhere indoors did get a bit muddy.

Towards the end of the month we were given the keys to the house which was to become our retirement home for over 30 years. We called it 'Clarehaven' after the lovely hotel at Bognor where we had spent so many happy family holidays. The house needed a lot of work to make it acceptable and we had to decorate throughout, so we spent most of September and October working flat out. We also managed to fit in a visit to the farm by Stephane, Kristine and Grandpa Augustin from Normandy. Grandpa had never been out of France. He wanted to see the Major Oak (the French all seem to love the legend of Robin Hood) and Nottingham Castle, so we had a few outings with them.

On November 1st we moved out of the farm – it was a very sad day. We had spent nearly thirty years there and brought up our three sons. David and Edward had been born in the old farmhouse which was large and full of character, but very damp. It had been pulled down in 1961 ready for our current farmhouse which had been built on the same site. We were leaving the farm but another chapter in our lives was just beginning.

Chapter 22

RETIREMENT (1988)

1988 brought significant changes to our lifestyle. Farming was behind us but we were renting what had been a smallholding at the opposite end of Rolleston. This had a full set of farm buildings and three and a half acres of land. We chose not to keep any animals so that we could go away when we pleased. The garden was large and very overgrown with nettles and horseradish, just the sort of challenge I liked. We still had a small tractor, so we dragged the garden away from the house and left a large heap at the far end which eventually rotted down, but it took years to get rid of the horseradish.

I spent a lot of time sowing lawns, planting borders and growing vegetables. Dick made himself a small workshop and took up joinery again. He had been apprenticed as a joiner when the war started and he had to enlist. He made a lot of items for the house and garden.

Inside the house we had moved the bathroom upstairs which had doubled the size of the kitchen. The living room fireplace was small and out of alignment so the boys put a new stone one in. All ten internal doors had had plywood nailed over both sides. This was removed to reveal pine doors which had been painted. We had them all stripped and then waxed, which showed off the pine to its best advantage. There were still jobs to be done inside but they were mostly cosmetic.

We had brought with us our 18' x 10' cedar wood sun lounge from the farm. Dick and I had dismantled it section by section (they were bolted together) one Sunday afternoon, and loaded the sections onto a trailer to tow down the road to our new residence. The boys removed an old shed attached to the back of the house and re-assembled it there on a new concrete base.

They put on a new roof and gave the wood-work a coat of preservative and we are still using it regularly over thirty years later. The landlord had offered us £150 to leave it behind but we had bought it fifteen years earlier; it was ours and we knew we could still benefit and get enjoyment from it.

The year turned out to be quite a family orientated year. David and Sarah went to Paris for a weekend to meet up with Stephane, and whilst there got engaged. David bought the engagement ring in Paris, but rumour has it that he didn't pluck up the courage to 'pop the question' until they were halfway home on the 'plane!

Peter and Denise moved to a house at Barnstone, having spent the first four years of married life at Balderton. Luke celebrated his first birthday in May and a week later baby Matthew joined his brother. We had some very happy times that summer with the two little ones, and there were parties galore at Denise's parents' lovely home at Thoroton.

We managed just a long weekend in Normandy on a coach taking some of Dick's comrades. We joined in the usual celebrations at Flers and stayed for three nights with Jean and Monique.

The parish said goodbye to our lovely vicar, Norman Todd, and his wonderful family of seven. He had been an inspiration to us all. The younger children had played with ours, and many others, almost daily and I became Godmother to their youngest, Sarah. We were all sorry to see them go but we have always kept in touch.

In July we spent a weekend with Norman and Beryl at Kidlington, from where we attended the wedding of Jeanne and Giles. The following month they visited us to attend the wedding of Helen and Anthony, both girls being the daughters of Dick's cousins Margaret and Ruth. Dick had spent a lot of time with his cousins in his younger days when they all went camping and caravanning at Woodham Ferrers in Essex, and they were always a very close-knit family.

In September I went off to the Lake District with my four special friends from the art class. We rented our teacher Marjorie's house at Applethwaite near Keswick for a week. It was built into the hillside below Skiddaw Mountain and offered spectacular views from the upper floor. There was a mezzanine gallery with an unusual staircase, each stair being the size of just one foot. We did lots of painting and sketching, and visited local places of interest such as craft demonstrations and small art galleries. As usual we sampled half a dozen different pubs or hotels for our evening meals.

Soon after my return home our French friends Jean and Monique from Normandy came to stay. We took them to places of interest and visited friends and family who were spreading out across the area now. This time around we had a fine day in Derbyshire when the trees were at their most colourful.

In mid-November Norman and Beryl came again for the weekend of baby Matthew's Christening.

Chapter 23

CELEBRATIONS & HOLIDAYS GALORE (1989-1990)

1989 proved to be a good year with my efforts at painting – mostly in oils but the odd watercolour too. I had a couple of commissions, both of horses. As I am not a horse rider, I found this quite a challenge as every muscle on the equine body seems to stand out and must be painted accurately. Otherwise the poor beast looks like anything but a horse. Anyway, the recipients were satisfied and I was off to the shop to spend my earning on more paints. I also painted two boats and a Cairn Terrier as presents. However, landscapes remain my favourite and of course flowers are close behind.

In April Gwen, Doris, Dorothy and I went off to Bath again for a week to do more painting and sketching. The house was on a hill overlooking the town, and one evening we were sitting quietly when a hot air balloon went past our window. It landed in a field opposite.

We had a plethora of parties that year. Luke and Matthew were two and one respectively; David and Sarah were married in Southwell Minster followed by a reception for about sixty at Kelham Hall; Dick celebrated his 70th birthday with a big family barbeque in our garden. Cousin Victor had invested in a fantastic cine camera and took some fabulous film of the occasion. These barbeques continued year on year until Dick's 98th birthday. After his death the close family decided they wanted to continue the tradition, and so we celebrated what would have been his 100th birthday in the usual way.

The final party that year of '89 was David's 30th, which was a surprise party held at the Admiral Rodney in Southwell for which I made a cake resembling his boat 'Misty Morn'.

Meanwhile we had had a weekend in Normandy for an army re-union, when a quite memorable Sunday lunch was provided in the village of Tinchbray-Bocage.

We also spent a week in the Lake District with Norman and Beryl staying at Marjorie Arnfield's house in Applethwaite. We enjoyed quite a few walks at Derwentwater, Bassenthwaite, Borrowdale and Seathwaite where we watched sheep being sheared. We then drove over Honister Pass to Buttermere where we took most of the day to walk round the lake. Wordsworth's Dove Cottage at Grasmere was most enjoyable as was a visit to Beatrix Potter's home, Hill Top Farm at Sawrey. We also visited Hawkshead to see an exhibition of her sketches. The last day was spent at the famous Ashness Bridge and Watendleth Tarn, where we had afternoon tea in the courtyard of the farm with chaffinches eating crumbs from our hands.

In September we flew out to Majorca where Mr Radford's motor boat 'Dogger' was berthed. He had very kindly offered us a week on it, so seven of us jumped at the chance. Dick and I, David and Sarah, Sarah's parents and Eddie came too. We were moored at Port d'Andratx to the west of Palma and we found a different bay each day to anchor, and swim from the boat. We only went ashore to do food shopping or treat ourselves to an evening meal. David of course was the qualified 'skipper' but we each had a go on the wheel. The weather was perfect all week. It had been a real treat!

In 1990 Dick and I went to stay with Barbara and Reg at Worthing for Easter. They were keen gardeners and took us to some lovely gardens and nurseries, among them Ingwersen's who specialise in alpine plants. This was very colourful and much to my taste. We spent an afternoon in the pretty and quaint town of Arundel, full of top-quality antique shops. Up on the South

Downs we re-visited the Weald & Downland open–air museum, where a vast number of ancient houses and buildings, retrieved from all over the UK, have been re-built and restored. It had expanded considerably since our first visit with the boys in the 1960s.

In April I was back in Bath with my art class friends, visiting old haunts such as Laycock, Castle Combe and Longleat, not to mention lunch at the famous Pump Room and tea at Sally Lunn's – both popular landmarks in the town. We didn't sit still for long. We were off to stay with Norman and Beryl again. They took us to the Cotswold Farm Park and Abingdon-on-Thames as well as many more pretty villages such as Burford, Great Rissington, and Bourton-on-the-Water.

In August we drove south to explore Dorset and more of Hampshire. Here we discovered a delightful bed & breakfast in a lovely thatched cottage at Buriton. We stayed a few nights and returned to this lovely spot several times in the next few years, on one occasion taking my best friend Madge with us and on another trip, we took Dick's sister Mary.

December brought some excitement which we could have done without. Overnight on the 7th we had very heavy snow and a strong easterly wind making conditions deplorable. We were woken by the wind lashing at our bedroom window, together with snow which stuck like glue and built up over half the window. There were flashes of light every few seconds from Staythorpe Power Station which was just across the fields opposite. At 6:45 am on the 6th December the power went off and wasn't restored for eight days! Power cables had been brought down all along the Trent Valley with the weight of the snow. All week we watched helicopters pick up and carry poles and cables to dump them, presumably, at the power station. Luckily we had an open fire and a camping gaz cooker, so we kept reasonably warm and cooked hot meals using up as much food as possible from our freezer, as the rest was spoiled. We always kept a supply of candles which were invaluable. Not everyone was so lucky. We had friends ring up and beg to come and sit by our fire! I have always respected the Scout motto 'Be Prepared'.

Shortly afterwards Eddie and Caroline got engaged calling for more celebrations.

My lifelong friend Madge came to stay for New Year as usual and we played Rummikub well into the early hours of the next morning. This became the norm now that we could have a lazy New Year's Day.

The last few weeks of 1990 I had been helping Ken Merryweather take cuttings of Cupressus Leylandii, a job right up my street. I was to return to help him in the New Year.

Chapter 24

CARRY ON HOLIDAYING (1991-1992)

In January and February of 1991 I was back helping Ken to complete his cuttings. In all I took 26,400 cuttings which were put into poly-tunnels, and misted automatically until well-rooted. Many people would have considered this boring but my green fingers found it most enjoyable and rewarding. Occasionally during the football season we were invited by my cousin Joan's husband, Clifford, to join them for lunch at the Notts County football ground to watch the match from his Executive Box. This was a real treat especially for Dick with his great love of football.

That spring we had heavy snow lasting for ten days, but the weather improved in time for a visit to the Lake District in April, again with Norman and Beryl, and staying in Applethwaite once more. We discovered new walks at Thirlmere, Ullswater (and Aira Force in Matterdale), Wastwater and Wasdale Head and we scrambled up the Lodore falls in Borrowdale.

In June Edward and Caroline were married at Rolleston followed by a reception at Colwick Hall. The previous day I had got up at 3am to accompany Caroline's Aunty Mavis to buy the flowers for the wedding at Nottingham's Wholesale Market, and spent the rest of the day decorating the church and making table decorations.

Then in July, David and Sarah's baby girl Sophie was born – our first granddaughter.

At this time there were a number of coach holidays and day trips advertised by various companies. They were very reasonably priced and usually between five and eight days long. During the next two decades we took advantage of these holidays to visit parts of the British Isles hitherto unknown to us, plus a few in Europe and Scandinavia. In all we partook of 35 such breaks, sometimes with friends but usually just the two of us. We made many more friends and sampled some excellent hotels, as well as seeing some wonderful countryside.

The first of these was a trip to Yorkshire to the areas where two current TV programmes had been filmed – Last of the Summer Wine where we were shown Norah Batty's house and the famous cafe etc., and the second was to 'Emmerdale' where we had drinks at the 'Woolpack Inn'. Ten days later another coach trip took us to the Northumbrian Coast to Bamburgh Castle, Seahouses and the island of Lindisfarne.

In early September the sea and the beach at Bognor beckoned once more, so we booked in at a bed & breakfast and covered some of our old stomping grounds, visiting friends and relatives while in the area, with the Royal Horticultural Show at Wisley added in. On our way home we stayed with Norman and Beryl for three nights. They took us to Avebury Circle one day and the next to the pretty village of Minster Lovell to watch a cricket match, where we had a picnic lunch beside the River Windrush. I remember someone hit a 'six' which landed in the river! Next morning we had trouble with the car and had to be relayed home by the AA.

On Caroline's birthday we all had dinner at the Black Swan at Beckingham near Newark where to my surprise the chef was Anton – one of my former Scouts! He was married to the daughter of the couple who owned the pub.

After the meal we had a long chat and he told me he had spent time in Switzerland, where he had been chef in a hotel at St. Moritz. While there he had bought a motorbike and toured the country on his days off. Later he had done the same in Scandinavia while a chef in Oslo. He then returned to a top

London hotel in order to prepare for his wedding. What an enterprising young man, I thought. I often wonder what happened to the rest of his fellow Scouts.

Perhaps learning to cook on wood fires at Scout camps inspired some lads to take up cookery as a career. Some time ago we learned that Darren, who was a contemporary of our three sons, became chef to Her Majesty The Queen at Buckingham Palace and subsequently to Prince Charles and Princess Diana.

In late September there was another weekend away with the art class, this time back to France to visit Monet's Garden at Giverny, where we spent a whole day sketching or painting in the garden and looking at the house. We stayed in Evreux which we explored, and finally returned to Paris to visit the Musée D'Orsay and L'Orangerie where a whole collection of Monet's waterlily paintings is exhibited. On our way home we stopped in Rouen to visit the cathedral, a painting of which became another of Monet's masterpieces.

The New Year followed our usual pattern. Madge came to our house to stay, friends over for dinner, Rummikub into the early hours and a healthy long walk on New Year's Day.

In the spring of 1992 I bought our first Peugeot 205 which was a very comfy car to drive, so off we went all over the country. First we went back to Bognor for a few days and then on to Barbara's at Worthing. While there we had some lovely walks in the bluebell woods and discovered a small garden at Wisborough Green owned by a sweet little elderly lady. She had some quite unusual plants for sale so Barbara and I were in our element. Further up the lane near her cottage was a sign 'Beware, Low Flying Ducks'. It was a very pretty spot and we returned many times. We also visited the village of Horsted Keynes which is twinned with the village of Cahagnes in Normandy where our French friends live. Before returning home we called to see one of Dick's army officers at Guildford. He and his wife were so welcoming, we were persuaded to stay the night. Next day we were off to Virginia Water to see Dick's cousin Don and his wife Pat in their lovely house that they had designed themselves. They had just added a large patio where we had a delicious cheese fondue lunch.

We were not in any hurry so we toured around a bit longer, staying at a farmhouse at Pishill in the Chilterns, where we explored even more beautiful countryside away from the main roads. We had taken the boys this way when they were young on our way to the south coast. They had thought the name of the village was hilarious, especially when the next village to it was called Bix Bottom. This soon took on a new name – Dad!

We were home for a short spell during which time we sowed our rather large front lawn.

It seemed prudent to support David in his latest boat-building enterprise, so we drove to Ipswich where he had a stand at the East of England Boat Show. We stayed in Harwich and toured around Constable Country to Dedham, East Bergholt etc. We called on another of Dick's army officers, Ted and his wife Jane, and were taken to see their sailing boat in the River Deben estuary. Later we heard nightingales in the hedgerows, and nightjars and a bittern booming on the marshes nearby. That was the only one I have ever heard. We drove the next day via Orford Ness, Bressingham Gardens and Thetford Forest – all new territory to us.

Soon after our return Emily Louise was born to Eddie and Caroline – our fourth grandchild.

Within a month we were back in Suffolk to spend a weekend on the sailing boat 'Bluster'. Ted and Jane were very keen sailors and had brought up four boys who all loved the sea, so the boat was well used. Ted had lost an eye and a hand in action during the war, and when sailing would wear a false hand with a hook for pulling up the anchor etc. Jane was an Admiral's daughter and had been well trained in all things nautical. We had nothing to fear, but where were the life jackets? "Oh, there are some pieces of

144

polystyrene in the cabin – we'll throw you one if you go overboard," was the answer! It was all very basic and Dick and I were offered a bunk in the cabin along with the portaloo. Our hosts slept under the stars. We had hot food. Jane cooked on a kind of camping stove with a pot on a gimbal so that it swayed with the boat and didn't spill – quite refined really – or so we thought. It soon became evident that there was a pig farm nearby and the wind was not in a favourable direction. We just had to move on but the water became shallower, and we took some time finding a suitable mooring without getting stuck in the mud.

Sunday morning was fine, luckily, as we had trouble with the engine and no amount of tinkering would get it going. Ted went off to find a marine engineer he knew (he seemed to know most people in the area!) It turned out that he had to bleed something to get it going. This done we set off and the engineer disappeared. When we stopped for lunch it happened again, so the engineer was summoned once more. He said we hadn't bled it long enough and set a time for doing it. From then on, each time we stopped Ted was able to bleed it himself, one of us timing him to the minute. This became known as 'The Bleeding Time'. The only problem was he had to keep disappearing into the bowels of the boat to rectify the problem. We spent some time looking around Snape and Aldeburgh before leaving the river and sailing out to sea. As I had been a Sea Scout Leader they insisted I had a go on the tiller. I had done some dinghy sailing on the river but never at sea and I was a bit nervous, but soon got the hang of it and thoroughly enjoyed it.

When it was time to return to the estuary Ted pointed out a sandbank – quite a famous one for getting marooned. So I handed the responsibility back to him and we returned to our mooring in the River Deben unscathed. Before we left to return home the next day, they invited us to join them on a trip to Holland (on the boat) later that summer. We politely declined knowing we hadn't the experience for such an adventure.

During July we had two more trips by coach, the first to Whitby and Goatland where we rode on the North Yorks Moors Railway. The second was to the Welsh Garden Festival at Ebbw Vale.

August found us looking after Luke and Matthew who were now 5 and 4 years old, so we took them swimming quite often, camped out in the garden and picnicked at a variety of favourite spots in Derbyshire. Sometimes we cooked lunch on a primus stove (probably baked beans!) near Ogston Reservoir where they could paddle and watch the sailing boats. One day we took them to the Tram Museum at Crich where we were able to ride on the top deck of the old trams, like the ones that had been in service during my childhood. They loved it.

When the school holidays were over we were free to take off again, so we set off for Scotland, staying in the Lake District en route for four nights exploring some yet unknown hills and valleys. Then on into Scotland to Aberfoyle and the Trossachs and to see Balquidder and Rob Roy's grave. I took Dick to show him the lush green valley where we had stayed when youth hostelling on our bikes. We crossed the bleak Rannoch Moor to Glencoe and to Fort William. While here I just had to show Dick where we had climbed Ben Nevis in 1950. We donned our boots and walked a little way up the footpath, having first crossed the river via the new footbridge. A little while later we spotted an eagle, a wonderful end to a perfect day. Our next stop was Oban and then on to Inverary, before driving through the Tweed Valley to Melrose. Next day we drove the 270 miles home in thick fog most of the way.

Our last jaunt of the year was to the Cotswolds, specifically to see the wonderful autumn colours of the Acers (Maples) at Westonbirt Arboretum as this was the last week of October. They were fabulous. I had never before seen such brilliant reds, oranges and yellows and all in one place. We stayed in Slad, the pretty village where Laurie Lee lived and made famous by his book Cider with Rosie, which most children read in school at some point. The town of Stow-on-the-Wold was also interesting with its wonderful array of antique shops.

The end of December was very cold, frosty and foggy and it remained so for two whole weeks without a let up, well into the New Year. New Year's Eve ended as usual with Rummikub played until the early hours and we managed our January 1st long walk, well wrapped up against the elements.

Chapter 25

TULIPS IN HOLLAND & SWITZERLAND REVISITED (1993)

1993 began quietly but revved up in March to become a very busy year. The winter was spent painting, and sowing seeds ready for the sale of plants in spring. There were two one day outings, one to the Royal Academy in London and one to the fine city of York.

In March we had a few days in Bath with Doris who showed us the 'must see' sights, as it was Dick's first visit. We enjoyed a day at Stourhead and again at Longleat. When we parked in the village of Horningsham Dick said, "I was stationed here in the army in that house next to the pub." So we lunched at the pub. We returned home via Tetbury and Batsford Arboretum.

In April we returned to Hampshire and stayed in a bed & breakfast at Hambledon, owned by the great nephew of Sir Edwin Lutyens, the famous architect who designed the Cenotaph in Whitehall, The Queen's Dolls House and numerous large and important buildings all over the world. It turned out to be quite an interesting history lesson. We dined at the Bat and Ball Inn just outside the village. In the field opposite the Inn, the very first game of cricket ever was played. It was a lovely part of Hampshire, not far from Meonstoke where Dick had lived as a boy and had been to school. We have stayed with the Lutyens' on several occasions since. We carried on down to the south coast and stayed at a house in Bosham. where the harbour is tidal and at high water the road is impassable. On one occasion we emerged from the pub after lunch to find a very embarrassed young lady whose car was half submerged. She had parked on the hard and forgotten about the incoming tide. She told us she lived locally and had no excuse. It cost her £25 to have the car towed to dry land and then had to get an engineer out before she could drive it again. When the boys were young, whilst we were on our summer holidays at Bognor we would often spend half a day at Bosham and would always make a point of driving around the perimeter road. It must have been the first time when young Edward commented, "Mummy look at all those knitted roofs," for there were dozens of pretty thatched cottages in the area. He was reminded of that observation for many years to come.

Soon after our return we went off on a five-day coach trip to Holland to visit the bulb fields and Keukenhof Gardens. We stayed near the village of Nunspeet in a wooded area, rather like Sherwood Forest, of mostly Silver Birch trees. In addition to a day at the famous Gardens which were very colourful, we visited Van Rozen's Nurseries where we were able to buy bulbs to be sent home. We crossed the Zuider Zee to a cheese farm at Edam to sample and buy, visited the lovely harbour of Volendam and spent a whole day in Amsterdam including a canal boat trip. We called at Bruges for the afternoon on the way home. Here we indulged in waffles and home-made chocolates.

One week back home and Scotland called again, this time on a coach trip, staying at Arrochar. We were privileged to be allocated the only bedroom on the top floor of a tall hotel, with only the lift and the viewing room for company. We made a lot of friends, as most people came up to look at the views which were spectacular in all directions. From here we visited Rothesay on the Isle of Bute and had a day in Rothesay sightseeing and then shopping in Edinburgh.

Soon afterwards we had a weekend with my nephew Tony and his wife Sharon at their lovely home at Newmarket. We were treated to a ride in Tony's vintage Jaguar to visit Ely.

In July we had another super holiday to Switzerland by coach, staying at Ghent, Strasbourg and a top-class hotel in Davos en route. We joined the Glacier Express to Andermatt via Landquart amid snow clad mountains, to rejoin the coach at Devil's Elbow and so on through the Susten Pass to Interlaken where we stayed for five nights. We had met Vera and Alan on the first day. They too were farmers and were celebrating their Ruby wedding, so we enjoyed their company for the rest of the holiday.

One day we visited the Alpine Gardens at Schynige Platte, which were stupendous in themselves, but with the added bonus of magnificent views across to the Jungfrau, the Monch and the Eiger. Another day we saw the wonderful wood carvings at Brienz and the pretty village of Meiringen. The Trumelbach Falls were even more spectacular than usual in torrential rain, but a party of Japanese visitors seemed unperturbed as they traipsed around without coats or umbrellas, and some were wearing flimsy high-heeled shoes. We passed the afternoon in the lovely mountain village of Grindelwald where I had previously stayed with my American relative. We finished the day off being treated to tea at the Metropole Hotel in Interlaken by Alan and Vera as it was their 40th wedding anniversary that day. Our final outing was a steamer trip the length of Lake Thun where we photographed lots of pretty villages. After an overnight stop in Liège we made for home and were told by our driver we had covered 2,000 miles.

A family holiday in Wales had been booked for the first week in August in a large house at Puncheston, Pembrokeshire. The family drove there on the Saturday, but Dick and I had been invited to Tim and Jill's wedding so we followed a day later. We enjoyed a day at Whitesand Bay and the lovely town of St. Davids with its historic cathedral. Next day we found the little fjord at Solva and Porthclais Harbour. On our way back to the house we came across a Scout Fete so we called in, and Luke and Matthew had a great time on the climbing wall and assault course. Tenby was our chosen destination the next day but it rained heavily so we all got a bit wet.

We went to see the reservoir and dam at Llan y Fam, this was educational but not very exciting on a children's seaside holiday. Next day we found a nice beach at Newgale and David tried out a windsurfer a friend had loaned him, much to the amusement of us all. The children also enjoyed a farm museum where they could hold the small animals and we made good use of the local swimming pool.

I had always wanted to explore the Welsh Marches, so on our way home Dick and I stopped for a couple of nights near Hay-on-Wye and visited Presteigne and Knighton, and sampled a piece of Offa's Dyke. I wish now that we had returned to walk the length of it.

In October we visited our ex-neighbours Jen and Gordon in their lovely home in Dorset. They took us to Shaftsbury and Heale House and Gardens and lots of other pretty villages. Before returning north we stayed with the Lutyens' again in order to re-visit some of our favourite spots like Mudeford, Buckler's Hard, Buriton and the Queen Elizabeth Country Park nearby.

Our year ended with a five-day break at Centre Parcs in Sherwood Forest with David, Sarah and 2-year-old Sophie.

Chapter 26

NORMANDY REUNION, CAMPING & 'LES POTS' (1994)

The first half of 1994 was spent at home, entertaining friends and family for the day or a dinner party in the evening. As the weather improved, we regularly took elderly relatives and friends out for a pub lunch, often into Derbyshire. They really enjoyed these outings.

When June arrived it was time to set off to France again. On the ferry to Caen we met Ted and Jane from Suffolk who were also on their way to the 11th Armoured Division reunion. We drove via Pegasus Bridge and had coffee together at Café Gondrée, the famous house beside the Bridge where in 1944 Monsieur and Madame Gondrée had brought out lots of hidden wine to celebrate their liberation. We visited the old museum there and saw the spots where each of the gliders had landed in the early hours of D-Day. There is a new museum now which is well worth a visit. It tells the story of the capture of the Bridge which was so vital to the progress of the troops.

Our arrival at Cahagnes, the home of Jean and Monique, was in time for aperitifs before the somewhat substantial evening meal, to which friends had been invited. On this occasion it was Jean-Pierre and his wife Therese, to whom we were introduced and whom we met on several subsequent visits. They owned the village charcuterie and Jean-Pierre also had a mobile shop which he took to various local markets. They had two teenage sons. The families were very close friends.

On Saturday morning Jean and Monique took us to Flers to the D-Day reunion where Dick met up with a number of his comrades. Once assembled, the 11th Armoured Division marched through the town to the town's memorial for a service with the mayor and other dignitaries. They then marched down the hill to the château where we had lunch and were shown round the museum. In the afternoon we were taken to the Perrier Ridge where a big battle had taken place. Here a memorial was unveiled in the village of Vassy. Afterwards we partook of Vin d'Honneur in the village hall. It had been an extremely hot day and we all got rather sunburnt.

On Sunday there was the usual service at the 11th Armoured Division Memorial just outside Flers, near the village of St. George des Groseillers (gooseberry bushes)! We followed the comrades to a lovely new sports hall where we had a most fabulous banquet. The houses were all decorated with flags and bunting, and many residents were outside applauding the men. Everyone was tremendously welcoming. It's very moving to see how much the French love our old soldiers and they cannot say "Thank you for 1944," enough. The band of the 3rd Royal Tank Regiment played after the meal and a young sergeant played wonderful solos on a very large xylophone. Later they made space for us to dance. It had been a wonderful day of comradeship.

The next day we went to the village of St. Martin des Besaces where the school children entertained us. They showed us their exhibition of D-Day pictures and presented each of the comrades with small English and French flags they had made, and they too said, "Thank you for 1944." We realised how much French children were being taught about the war in the hope it wouldn't happen again. We thought it was something our British youngsters lacked – but then our country wasn't occupied by the enemy. In recent years more has been taught in Britain about this very important part of our history. Later that day the men were awarded a French medal in appreciation of their contribution to the liberation of Normandy.

We went off on our own on Tuesday to find the town of Sées which is twinned with Southwell and has a cathedral not unlike our own Minster. It's a very attractive town and we could have spent longer exploring. On our way back we called at Bagnoles de l'Orne, a very pretty spa resort. It was very hot again – we could have done with a dip in the Orne but settled for ice creams (or so we thought). When they came, they were the biggest fruit sundaes we had ever seen – delicious!

On Wednesday we went to the market at Villers-Bocage where Monique bought a live cockerel, as is their usual practice. On the way back to their house we stopped to have aperitifs with some friends and as we were about to leave, Jean opened the car boot and the cockerel escaped! We all spent some time chasing it round their friends' lovely garden before it was re-captured.

On Thursday we went back to St. Martin des Besaces to see the newly-opened war museum. At a later date Dick presented to the curator the original copy of the 75th Anti-Tank Regiment Diary. We had a copy made by Stephane's friend who was a bookbinder in Paris which we still have. In the afternoon we were taken to the small village of Le Bény Bocage which saw some fierce fighting in 1944. It was near here that Dick's tank and the rest of the battery had sheltered in an orchard. He said the German bullets had come thick and fast and sounded like apples falling off the trees. They got one in the radiator of their tank which put it out of action for a few hours.

By Friday we had been at Cahagnes for a week, and had had a wonderful time being extremely well fed (and watered!) and taken all over the surrounding area. It was time to say farewell and set out on our drive to the Charente Maritime département, where we were going to stay at my nephew Tony's house for a further week.

It was again extremely hot but we had a good map and used part country roads and part motorway. While crossing the bridge at Angers the car engine overheated and we had to pull onto the hard shoulder. Some road workers kindly contacted the rescue service as we were in a hazardous position. It was blazing hot so they helped us push the car a little way to be in the shade of a rather small tree.

Once the engine cooled down we were off to find an overnight stop, which wasn't easy on a Friday. Eventually a hotel proprietor phoned a friend, in a village we had already passed through, who had a room. So we returned to the Cheval Blanc whose owner stood on the doorstep waiting to welcome us. He showed us our room and made us a meal. There was a big party in another room which went on till 3am. As it was so hot all the windows were open so it was very noisy. But we didn't mind, we were glad of a bed. I remember saying to Dick, "We didn't ask the price, but I don't care how much they charge," we were so tired after our hot and eventful day. The cost was in fact very reasonable.

Next day we were well on our way and decided on a picnic lunch in a farmer's field. Guess what! The car wouldn't start again. We pushed it into the shade and waited another hour and we were in luck. So we continued our journey without stopping, until we reach Tony's bungalow which is outside the village of Cercoux with only a farm and some derelict cottages nearby.

It was in a lovely spot with a pretty front garden and a lawn at the back where we could put up a gazebo and have a barbecue. The weather was perfect all week so we had most of our meals al fresco. There was a small vineyard behind the property, and at the front the view was extensive, with a pond in a hollow where we could hear the frogs croaking at night.

The small hotel in the village seemed the right place for Sunday lunch but there was a large birthday party in progress. However, when the proprietor was told we were 'Les Anglais' from Les Potiers, we were made very welcome and he found us a table. We had a very nice lunch.

On Monday morning we contacted the local garage and they very obligingly replaced the thermostat in the car. Nothing seems any trouble to the French.

Later we shopped in the local town of Coutras. The next day we drove to the lake at Montendre and picnicked on one of the sandy beaches. It was a safe place where children were paddling and sailing their boats. We drove back through extensive forests, falling in love with the countryside and the very pretty villages.

We ventured further afield on Wednesday as far as the coast, which was actually the estuary of the River Gironde. We visited the Citadel at Blaye and the medieval village there and had a meal in the garden of a lovely hotel. The local town of Guîtres was interesting and we had a picnic lunch beside the river there the next day.

On Friday it was time to leave Tony's and drive back north to the Vendée area on the Atlantic coast. Here we had booked an excellent campsite at Notre Dame de Monts. What a lovely area of pine forests and superb beaches. Many times during the week we walked down the sandy track through the forest to swim in the sea. We noticed that on Sunday whole French families gathered together for an alfresco lunch, commandeering one or two picnic tables of which there were many in among the trees. They had brought everything – even a whole cooked chicken and of course numerous bottles of wine. They do know how to enjoy themselves. Further along the coast at the beach near the little town of Notre Dame there was kite flying and model helicopters. At one of the small cafés we frequented, we were teased about our love of a cup of tea mid-afternoon while everyone else drank coffee or wine. One day we crossed the bridge to the island of Noirmoutier where we had lunch and watched the fishing boats unload crabs and lobsters.

We were sorry to leave this lovely campsite after twelve days but our holiday was not over yet. We had promised to go back to Jean and Monique's for a weekend before returning home. We broke the journey at Carnac for two nights and arrived to find an urgent message to ring home. My heart raced! But we had unknowingly left Tony's bungalow with the key to the bathroom window. His friends had arrived to find an unbearably hot bathroom in which they had gone to fit a new tank. Phew! We promptly posted the key back to them.

We were not enthralled with Carnac. The site was large and packed with tents far too close together, and the beach was filthy. We carried on to Cahagnes to find more excitement there. Monique's cousin's son was getting married the next day and we were invited to the reception which was a lavish affair. While in the vicinity we saw the village of Cheux where Dick's Regiment had fought a battle and we saw there were numerous bullet holes in the church walls. There was no let-up from the intense heat, so on the Sunday the family decided on a day at the coast at Coudeville-sur-Mer where their younger son David had a small caravan. We took lots of food and Stephane, the elder son, towed his boat there. After lunch it was time for some excitement. The boat was prepared and water skis attached. The two brothers took it in turns to ski while the other steered the boat. Dick and I were invited for a ride out. Dick and I had to hang on for dear life, it was so fast! I have never seen Dick look so scared and I didn't feel too good either.

We had to ask them to stop and drop us off. Dick looked uncomfortable for the rest of the day. We drove back to Cahagnes but there wasn't time for a meal, so Jean led us to Ouistreham ferry port and treated us to a meal in a restaurant. We got in the queue for the midnight ferry to Portsmouth. By now Dick's face was the colour of beetroot - he obviously had heat stroke and begged me to find a cabin where he could sleep. On arrival at Portsmouth all he wanted was a cup of tea so we found a small café. He could hardly keep his head up.

We had planned to visit a comrade's widow and he was determined to do so, but we went on a wild goose chase as she had moved to a nursing home. We couldn't find her and decided it was time to head for home. I was very worried about Dick as I was sure his blood pressure was sky-high. Once home he went straight to bed but recovered miraculously next day. (Only afterwards did I learn that someone with heat stroke should drink copious amounts of water - not tea!) So ended our wonderful 32-day holiday, which had been - to say the least - a bit on the hot side.

In July we had a day trip to Sandringham for the flower show which was excellent. We saw Prince Charles and the Queen Mother close enough to get some good photographs.

In September we made a return visit to Centre Parcs for 5 days along with David, Sarah and Sophie. Then in November we had a week-long coach holiday with our friends Mick and Sylvia to Ballater in the Scottish Highlands. We visited Braemar and Crathie Church as well as spending a whole day in Aberdeen with its very busy harbour. That concluded another exciting year.

Chapter 27

A NEW SPORT! NORWAY FOR OUR 40th ANNIVERSARY (1995)

The winter months of 1995 were again spent entertaining friends and family. We had snow and then floods and in general, very low temperatures.

In April Dick and I went to London to a reunion at the Victory Services Club where we met comrades from some of the other army regiments. We spoke to a Welshman who had spent a weekend's leave with a pal whose home was in Rolleston. His host was the son of the couple who had farmed at The Croft before we took it over. What a small world it is!

At Easter we went to Worthing again and Barbara and Reg took us to several new venues, notably the village of Bramber which had two museums, a butterfly museum and one where everything connected with smoking was displayed. It was interesting but smelly, we didn't stay long! We had a nice walk by the river there and another in Ashdown Forest near where my Godson, Chris, lives. Before heading for home, we just had to re-visit Bognor and Bosham and discovered the lovely village of Rowland's Castle with its splendid village green. After a night on a farm at West Meon we toured the extensive Queen Elizabeth Country Park and finished up reminiscing at Meonstoke.

Back home we took up a new interest. We began playing short mat bowls in the village hall along with a number of friends. This we continued to play for about twenty years. We also played outdoors at Southwell, and indoors there in the winter, for several years on Saturday afternoons.

Norman and Beryl came for the weekend of our 40th wedding anniversary in May and we had a big party with family and friends at the Olde England Hotel at Sutton-on-Trent. Our main celebration was a coach holiday in Norway along with Vera and Alan, the friends we had made on the Swiss holiday two years previously. It was Dick's first visit to Norway and it turned out to be a super nine-day trip. The coach driver's wife was courier. She was an excellent guide and had a lovely personality. She kept us entertained and she and Dick hit it off at once. They used to have a little dance together before we set off each morning. The first was on the quayside at Bergen. If it was raining, they danced up and down the gangway in the coach much to everyone's amusement. We spent some time in Bergen looking at the Hanseatic houses with their museums and historic buildings and the Bryggen, a maze of characteristic buildings - all very colourful. After a visit to the fish and flower markets we took the funicular railway up to Mt. Floyen where there are lots of footpaths through the woods. It was here that Barbara and I had stayed at the youth hostel back in 1953.

Next day our journey took us to Hardanger Fjord with its lush green banks of orchids and many other wild flowers, and the dense blossom of apple and cherry trees, all set against a background of towering Blue Mountains and thundering waterfalls. It was really stunning scenery. We crossed by ferry to the charming village of Norheimsund and on to Granvin where we had lunch. This was a village of traditions and culture, and from the coach we saw a large timber business in operation with multiple huge piles of sawdust. We continued our journey to Voss and just beyond to our hotel at Oppheim for two nights.

Next day we had a special excursion, one of the highlights of the holiday. At Voss we took the main Bergen-Oslo train to Myrdal, a station high up on the Hardanger Plateau to connect with the famous Flam funicular railway, one of the steepest in the world. The train winds its way down a narrow glacial valley with wild and beautiful scenery, stopping frequently for passengers to take photographs, especially of the massive waterfalls. The quiet village of Flam sits on the edge of Aurlandsfjord, and has a purpose-built tourist centre where we had time to browse before joining our coach to return to our hotel via the seven-mile-long Gudvangen Tunnel. As well as the road down to Flam there is a footpath and cycle track.

The following year the courier Alison wrote to tell us she had walked down to Flam as she had always wanted to do.

We left Oppheim to follow the Adventure Road across Norway in the direction of Oslo, but first we called at the Stalheim Hotel for coffee. I had first been there in 1953 on my youth hostelling holiday with Barbara, but that particular hotel had been built of timber and had burnt down. The new hotel is much bigger and more sophisticated. It stands in a very imposing position at the head of the Naerodal Canyon, the road down beginning with sixteen zig-zags and carrying on to Gudvangen. We had walked it in 1953. There is a magnificent view of the Canyon from the hotel with huge snow-capped peaks on either side. In the garden there is still a concrete German lookout post.

We took the ferry from Gudvangen to Revsnes passing through Norway's narrowest fjord, Naeroyfjord, where sheer cliffs reach down to the water's edge. We continued along Aurlandsfjord to Sognefjord – Norway's longest and deepest. At Revsnes we re-joined the coach and visited the charming and delightfully preserved village of Laerdal. The lovely houses were all built of wood and lots of them had small statues of trolls in their doorways. We next stopped at Borgund to see one of the country's oldest Stave churches. From there our journey took us up over miles of wild snow-covered uplands with no habitation, only the odd ski hut here and there. We went through Hemsedal and onto Gol – where I had camped with the Scouts in 1975. This time I had the luxury of a lovely bed in a luxurious en-suite room, rather than a tent!

We left the hotel the next morning to drive through the beautiful Hallingdal valley passing some very large lakes with unpronounceable names. We had left the mountains behind. Our last morning was spent touring the beautiful city of Oslo and in the afternoon, we visited the Vigeland Sculpture Park and the Olympic ski jump at Holmenkollen from which there are impressive views over Oslo. That evening we joined a ship for an overnight crossing to Denmark, and were then taken by coach through the heart of the country to the port of Esjberg for our final overnight crossing to Newcastle. It had been a fabulous holiday, and Dick took Norway to his heart the same as I had done in 1953. What wonderful people and what a beautiful country it is!

In June we were invited to join Norman and Beryl in a cottage at Leyburn in Wensleydale, Yorkshire for a week. They had been there before and knew where to show us the best scenery and places of interest. These included the Aysgarth Falls nearby, Bolton Abbey and the pretty villages of Askrigg, Bainbridge and Hawes. We followed the River Swale from the lovely town of Richmond to the attractive village of Reeth with its huge village green, which is a hive of activity on market day. We then went on to Gunnerside and Muker where wild flowers grew in abundance, and a whole hillside was covered with buttercups between there and Keld near the small hamlet of Thwaite. We drove up the Buttertubs Pass and stood on the rocks peering with trepidation into the enormous crevices below.

Another day we visited the ruins of Jervaux Abbey and Fountains Abbey with Studley Royal Water Garden which were of historical interest, as was the area near Reeth where tin had once been mined. We sampled the beer at the Tan Hill Inn which stands alone and is supposed to be the highest pub in Britain, complete with its own ghost! Hardraw Force was another spectacular waterfall and the church and old bridge at Hubberholme were worth a detour. We came home via Knaresborough which is a lovely old town with lots of history and some nice shops and eateries. It had been chosen by my parents for their honeymoon.

The hot weather continued right through July, three weeks of which was taken up with picking and freezing soft fruits from the garden.

August was no cooler and by now our glut of tomatoes, plums, and apples were ready for preserving or freezing. We had to buy another freezer! You may wonder why we didn't give some away or even sell them. Well, we tried but everyone had bumper crops of fruit that year.

The grandchildren were away on holiday so we played bowls on several occasions and we had a day out to Grimsby, to visit Peter Carr who served alongside Dick in the war. He had remained a single man and travelled a lot by motorbike. He especially visited the battlefields in Europe where they had fought, and he sought out families with whom the men in 117 Battery had been billeted in Holland. He did this for several years and made many, many friends. He called on us at the farm periodically to show us lots of photos he had taken on these trips. Peter had also taken cine films of his travels which he showed at the 117 Battery reunion each November in Manchester. These get-togethers happened every year until the Millenium.

When September arrived so did the rain, and the grandchildren too were back. So it was a bit of a mixed month with water-proofed and welly-clad children to entertain. But we survived!

As November remained relatively mild our friends Mick and Sylvia suggested a coach holiday to Cornwall, 'just to wrap up the year'. Well, why not? We stayed in St. Ives where most days felt like summer apart from the lack of tourists. Gardens were still colourful with bedding plants and there was hardly a ripple on the sea. Our coach driver commented how pleasant it was to be able to take us down country lanes without getting stuck in traffic. We visited Truro Cathedral, Falmouth and Penzance, always stopping off for coffee or lunch. We had a good look at the Minack open-air theatre near Land's End, and we also spent time in the Tate Gallery in St. Ives. Both Sylvia and I were members of an art class at that time.

In December we had our usual village outing to see the spectacular Christmas Show at Thursford, near Sandringham in Norfolk. This had become an annual event for us. It was held at the Steam Museum and was a musical and colourful show like no other. Performances were held all the way through December, matinees and evenings, and it was always fully booked. Our day out began with a coffee stop en route and we usually took a sandwich to eat on the coach before the 2pm performance. Dinner on our way home was pre-booked at a hotel. There was never a spare seat on our coach!

Chapter 28

SOGGY TEDDIES ON THE WATERCRESS LINE & ANOTHER SURPRISE IN NORMANDY (1996)

1996 began with typical wintry weather – fog, ice, lots of snow and very low temperatures, with stopovers by grandchildren and the usual spread of visiting friends. In March we went to Torquay with John and Marigold, the only holiday we ever had with them. There was one sunny day when we walked to the very pretty Cockington village. Other days we sought sheltered spots from the biting wind at lovely places like Paignton, Brixham, Teignmouth and Dawlish where we saw the famous black swans. At Dartmouth we braved a short boat trip on the river. Luckily there was a swimming pool at the hotel which Dick and I made good use of.

In the Easter holidays we took our two eldest grandchildren, Luke and Matthew, on an educational adventure. En route to Hampshire we stopped for a picnic lunch at Brill in Oxfordshire, where an old post-mill sits on a prominent hilltop with 360-degree panoramic views. Dick and I had stopped there many times, but what we hadn't realised was that the soil was clay and it had been raining. It was the ideal spot for small boys to explore the narrow paths among the gorse and grassy banks where sheep had grazed. To our horror they re-appeared covered in mud and we were booked into a Travelodge! We used our supply of drinking water to clean them up and set off again. When we were ready for a 'cuppa' we were nearing Henley-on-Thames and knew of a café with a car park near the river. Duly refreshed we had a walk along the riverside, stopping at the lock to join the other 'gongoozlas' watching the boats pass through. The boys thought this was great fun. On our way back to the car we were reading the names on seats donated in memory of loved ones. Matty said to me, "Does that say Goofy?" "No," I replied, "it says Geoffrey and it happens to be your middle name!" Well, he was only seven.

Our Travelodge for four nights was at Fourmarks near Alton in Hampshire. We had chosen this venue on the Watercress Line which runs between Alton and New Alresford and where, at Ropley, there are vast sheds housing a number of steam engines being restored by an army of volunteers. The line is so named because it used to transport tons of watercress grown in the area up to London. We spent a whole day riding up and down the line on Thomas the Tank Engine, James the Red Engine and Henry the Green Engine, stopping off for lunch in the pretty little town of New Alresford. These of course were the engines made famous in the books by the Reverend Awdry.

However, it rained, and it rained all day long. We had never seen so many sodden grandparents and grandchildren complete with soggy teddy-bears on a day out. The youngsters were undeterred by the weather, they had come to see their favourite engines and the Fat Controller, and they did!

Next came a very full day of historical interest at Portsmouth dockyard. After the obligatory visit to Nelson's flagship HMS Victory, we were given a tour of Britain's first iron-clad warship HMS Warrior, launched in 1860, complete with characters dressed in period costume, and they were very informative. We then entered a large building housing the Mary Rose, a Tudor warship recently raised from the seabed which was being misted constantly to keep it preserved. We were to get a reasonable view of it from a board walk. Our final visit of the day was to the Maritime Museum which was also very informative. The boys loved it. We finished up at Southsea, playing football on the wide grassy seafront in the evening sunshine.

As Dick was keen to show the boys where he had been brought up, we spent the following day touring the pretty villages of the Meon Valley – Meonstoke where he went to school and lived for a short while, Exton where he sang in the church choir and Corhampton where he lived for most of his childhood, and where he and his brothers had learnt to swim in the river at the bottom of the garden. We carried on to the coast at Bosham, a favourite spot of ours with its pretty tidal harbour and famous church where King Canute is supposed to be buried in the crypt. The boys were intrigued. We then drove on to Bognor Regis where we had spent over a dozen happy holidays when their father and uncles were young.

We returned home via Henley-on-Thames and spent more time with the gongoozlas at the lock. The boys had really enjoyed their Easter holidays. The rest of April and most of May were taken up with gardening -planting vegetables of all kinds and tidying up the flower borders which were quite colourful. We joined a couple of one-day coach outings from our village, one to Derbyshire taking in Hartington and Buxton and the other to the Humber Bridge, Hornsea Pottery and Bridlington.

In mid-June we set off for a two-week camping holiday at Piriac on France's west coast, the Loire-Atlantique region, but first we were bidden to Cahagnes to stay with Jean and Monique for a week, no army reunion on this occasion. We did however go via Pegasus Bridge and find the grave of Captain Crowther at Bannerville. His grave was the only one of Dick's comrades as yet undiscovered. On arrival at Cahagnes we were told we were being taken to a party on the Saturday. This was to celebrate the 30th birthday of Nathalie, Stephane's girlfriend, and it was to be held at an agricultural college north of Paris, 200 miles away, where the whole family would stay.

But first, on the Friday night was just another little surprise, a 'Son et Lumière' at Château de Chantilly in that same area. Naturally it took place in the dark so didn't begin until around 11pm and finished (yes, you've guessed it) about 2am. Next day was extremely hot and I had only taken party gear. We sat outside all day under the gazebos while the party was prepared indoors. My sandals got tighter and tighter and my skin got browner and browner. The party was excellent and went on well into the early hours, as is normal practice with the French. Most people slept until midday and then a football match was organised! 'Les Anglais' were included, but we had taken a limited amount of clothing and Dick was reluctant to play in his best suit and white shirt, but he played! Everyone else wore shorts, but no mention of this had been made to us before we set off, unless of course my understanding of French is not as good as I'd thought.

Next morning Monique left early with a cousin to attend a family funeral and Jean decided we would make a detour en route back to Cahagnes to visit the Basilica of St. Thérèse at Lisieux. This we really enjoyed as it was a beautiful place full of atmosphere and quite a moving experience.

In the next two days Jean and Monique took us to a number of places including the lovely coastal town of Courseulles-sur-Mer, and a village named Colleville to which the name of Montgomery had recently been added, and a statue of the famous Field-Marshall erected on the green.

We left Cahagnes on the Thursday to drive to our campsite at Piriac, stopping in the towns of Mortain and Fougéres to stretch our legs. The campsite was good and had all the facilities we needed, but there wasn't a lot going on, so we toured around the Loire-Atlantique area and discovered some lovely places like La Turballe which has a beach for bathing, Le Croisic with a huge marina full of boats and the pretty little resort of Batz-sur-Mer. We passed huge salt beds where women swept sea salt into enormous piles with a very long-handled type of broom.

On our return home most of July and August were spent picking and freezing soft fruits and beans. We had grandchildren to stay as usual and took them for a picnic in Derbyshire one day, and lots of trips to the swimming pool at Edwinstowe.

In September Jean and Monique came over from Normandy two days after the birth of David and Sarah's daughter, Lucy, so we had a family party in order for everyone to meet our guests and welcome the new baby. We took the visitors to Lincoln, Belvoir Castle and Papplewick Pumping Station which was of great interest to Jean. Monique enjoyed an exhibition at Rufford Country Park called 'Place Settings' as she loves cooking and entertaining.

October saw us on a five-day coach trip to the Isle of Wight, somewhere we hitherto had only ever been for a day. A lovely hotel in Shanklin provided excellent food and accommodation. The morning of market day was spent in Newport, the capital, and in the afternoon we visited Osbourn House and Swiss Cottage where Queen Victoria spent her holidays. The pretty village at Godshill was a must as was Freshwater and the famous Pearl Centre. Next came a ride on the chairlift at Alum Bay, with wonderful views of the Needles and across the Solent to Southampton and Portsmouth, and we couldn't leave without a boat trip to Cowes and Ventnor. We left the Isle of Wight the following day.

On the way home our coach broke down, the clutch had gone and we were transferred by a local coach to a motorway café, where we waited four hours for a replacement coach to be sent from Nottingham. Everyone was annoyed as our coach had been making a strange noise ever since leaving Nottingham five days earlier. There was no apology from the company despite our complaints. It was the only time we had ever had cause for complaint as generally coaches were in tip-top condition and very comfortable, we used eight or nine different companies over the years so we had been very lucky.

The rest of the year was taken up with grandchildren at half-term and then the usual run of Christmas Concerts and Nativity Plays at their various schools.

Chapter 29

YORK, MEONSTOKE & NORMANDY AGAIN (1997)

It snowed heavily after Christmas and into the New Year of 1997 and icy roads made driving difficult. February and March were fine and mild and I did a lot of gardening. In the Easter holidays we took Luke and Matthew to York for six days, staying in a Travelodge just outside the city. We saw pretty well every building that had a history and they both loved the Jorvik Centre. A whole day was spent at the Railway Museum and was greatly enjoyed. Around 4pm when I was about on my knees a little voice reminded me, "But Granny we haven't walked around the City Wall yet." So off we went on another gruelling hike.

Next day we went out to Eden Camp which depicts life during the Second World War. The boys were fascinated and Dick and I really enjoyed it too. On the way back we had tea in the pretty village of Helmsley. They had set their sights on the Armoury at Leeds so for a change we took the bus (top deck) to enjoy the view en route. It was a much larger venue than I had expected and by far the most expensive museum we had ever visited. It was not quite my cup of tea and Dick was non-committal, but the boys loved every minute of the day.

In May we had a day's outing from our village to Evesham, a smart little town set in a vale of hundreds of acres of cherry trees which were in full bloom – it was a wonderful sight.

A week later we set off for Meonstoke, this time taking Dick's sister Mary with us. She had been born there and liked to return periodically to reminisce with her brothers. We stayed with the Lutyens family again for two nights and had two further nights on a farm at East Meon. We visited the village school and spoke to a teacher whose mother had been at school with Dick. She directed us to her mother's house where we found her at home, next door to where Dick's family had lived. We found three more of his old school friends, two of whom we visited for several years whenever we were in the area. On our last day we met Norman and Beryl for lunch at the Bucks Head in Meonstoke and then drove up to a spot called Winchester Hill overlooking the village and far beyond out to sea. Unfortunately, we had both cars broken into while we'd gone for a walk. We contacted the police and were asked to meet them at Droxford, where we made a statement and finger prints were taken. Apparently car thieves were prevalent in the area and we heard no more. It did however mean a trip into Portsmouth on the Sunday morning to get a new rear window fitted before we could drive home in the rain.

June began badly with Dick not being very well and he spent two weeks in hospital with polymyalgia. He recovered well on medication, but the rest of the month was a washout as it rained for nine days out of twelve.
July improved considerably and we joined a day's coach outing from Rolleston to the Yorkshire Dales, made famous by All Creatures Great and Small.

August was even better and very hot at times. There was a three-day visit to Edinburgh by coach to see the Military Tattoo, which was spectacular on a lovely warm evening.

Eddie, Caroline and Emily were on holiday at Abersoch in the family's caravan and invited us to join them for a few days. We enjoyed lots of barbeques and they showed us around the Lleyn Peninsular and the picturesque Italianate village of Portmeirion. It was good to have the chance to play on the beach with 5- year-old Emily and in the sea with her little boat. En route home we stayed overnight in Llangollen and vowed to return there one day. Then we stopped off at Sudbury Hall to visit the Museum of Childhood which we found very interesting. The rest of the school holidays were spent at a variety of swimming pools with the grandchildren and lots of days out with a picnic.

When they were all back at school we set off for Normandy, but without the car. We took the National Express coach from Nottingham to London and then Portsmouth. We crossed on the ferry as foot passengers. Jean and Monique met the ferry at Ouistreham and we spent two most enjoyable weeks being entertained by them, and visiting lots of new places that were unknown to us. They took us in their camping car to the American landing beaches of Utah and Omaha, where thousands of American troops had lost their lives on D-Day and the days that followed. At the small town of St Mère Église there is an effigy of an American paratrooper who got hooked onto a small pinnacle on the church tower. While hanging there the bells were rung to warn of the invasion, and the poor chap was deafened and remained so for the rest of his life. He faked death at the time so that the Germans just left him there. It's not known how long he remained there before being rescued. At the small museum in the town, we noticed an English plane that had been based at RAF Balderton near Newark.

We visited Mt. Pincon, which is the highest point for miles around, and which was used by the Germans as a vantage point as they had a 360-degree view over the whole of Normandy. Dick had been there shortly after its capture as had my brother Harry who was in the 43rd Wessex Division.

A day in the Swiss Normande region was a welcome change from visiting battlefields. First, we were taken to a museum containing the largest model railway layout in Europe. It covers 310 square metres with 430 metres of track on which 16 trains run through various countries of Europe. There are 230 locomotives, 400 wagons, 1300 lorries and cars, 680 houses and more than 2,500 lights. We first saw it in daylight and then lit up at night. I was fascinated by the moving details such as a fairground, campsite, ice rink, football and tennis players, bandstand with dancers, the fire brigade extinguishing a fire, and police attending a traffic accident. Later we had lunch on the terrace at a lovely restaurant overlooking the river watching canoeists and other pleasure boaters. We visited two châteaux – one at Balleroy, where there was a hot air balloon festival and the other at Vendeuvre, where we saw a wonderful display of dolls' houses and their enormous collection of doll's house furniture. In the pretty gardens there were water fountains and other features which were activated as we approached and often gave us a soaking. Luckily it was a very hot day.

Another day out in the campervan was to the fairly newly constructed Pont du Normandie Bridge over the River Seine. It really is an enormous bridge and we were able to walk on it and take photos. We carried on to the lovely resort of Deauville where lots of film stars take their holidays and own beach huts. We then drove to the interesting port of Honfleur, returning home to Cahagnes via Pegasus Bridge.

After two very full weeks with Jean and Monique we returned to Portsmouth by ferry and then on to London by coach. As we had several hours to wait for the connecting coach home, we visited the Royal Mews to see the full range of royal carriages and horses and a brief look at the Queen's Gallery. We found the journey by coach more tiring than with the car and far less convenient.

In October we were back to a normal routine, numerous friends for the day, grandchildren at weekends, harvest festival and supper, dances and lots of indoor bowls, not to mention the garden always needing attention and a batch of market research to do in order to save for the next holiday. This came in November when we were invited to join friends on a five-day coach trip to Newquay. We had sampled their 'Christmas' breaks before and they were extremely good value for money, one day emulating Christmas Day and the next Boxing Day with the emphasis on food, games and competitions. There were also outings to Truro, Padstow, Crantock and St. Agnes with a visit to Redruth Tin Mine.

Once home our preparations were in full swing for Christmas. As usual the whole family were with us for Boxing Day, by now over a dozen of us to feed and then Madge came for New Year. Sadly, Norman had passed away earlier in the month and the boys took us to his funeral at Oxford in January.

Chapter 30

SNOWCOACH TO AUSTRIA & MOSELLE WINE HARVEST (1998)

The early part of 1998 was very mild, 19 degrees being recorded on the 14th February and 12 degrees at night on March 17th. That day we set off for Austria on the 'Snow Coach' holiday with our friends Mick and Sylvia. But it was mild there too and there was very little snow to be seen when we arrived. We had a very full day in Salzburg visiting all things 'Mozart' and enjoying already colourful gardens. Next day it was Vienna's turn to be explored. Furnished with a list of sights not to miss we set off for the Cathedral and the Ankeruhr Clock. Our coffee break was taken at McDonalds and as we came out, we were greeted with a loud clap of thunder and lightning and it was snowing hard, with huge flakes. We sheltered in the doorway for a while and then decided to brave it. We were soaked in no time and the pavements were awash with slush. We made for the Opera House but it was locked. Sylvia spotted a museum and suggested it would be warm and dry. The museum was all about Bhutan! A country I had never even heard of. The day was a complete washout and we were very disappointed.

As we left the capital on our coach, the authorities were hard at work carting lorry loads of snow and dumping it in a disused canal which had been left empty for this purpose, such was the regularity of this type of weather. For most of the trip back to our hotel a snowplough preceded us. Everywhere people were out cleaning pathways and already snow lay a foot deep on hedges and walls.

This all made the following day more exciting as we were taken to the pretty village of St. Gilgen, made even more attractive by the amount of snow that had fallen. A cable car took us to the top of the mountain from where we had stunning views, and where 3 feet of snow was being cleared to give us access to the café in order for us to have a coffee. Later we toured the lakes, stopping off at Mondsee, Traunkirchen and St. Wolfgang where we saw the famous White Horse Inn. We left Weyregg beside Lake Attersee after four days and travelled back via Munich where we had an afternoon to look around, and then drove through the centre of Brussels at night which was all lit up and quite a sight.

It was now April and we noted that we had been at Rolleston 40 years. In the Easter holidays we took Luke and Matthew back to Hampshire, this time encountering heavy snow en route and it was extremely cold for the next four days. We re-visited Meonstoke, Portsmouth and Southsea and went to see the submarines at Gosport, being allowed to go on one to appreciate the cramped conditions. Boxes of supplies filled the gangway and we had to crawl along them to reach the other end. The galley was exceptionally small and we wondered how on earth the cooks managed to feed the whole crew. No wonder they are accommodated in top class hotels when they do occasionally surface. One day we took the boys to see King Arthur's Round Table at Winchester along with the Military Museum and the beautiful cathedral.

Once back home we spent the next two weeks decorating the bedrooms, but had a day in Derbyshire in May on our wedding anniversary. We picnicked in Dovedale and had a long walk and tea in Ilam Country Park (memories of my first Youth Hostel) and finished the day with an excellent meal at The George at Alstonefield.

Most of June was spent gardening and entertaining friends but at the end of the month we went off back down to the southern counties. We first stayed with the Pitchers near Salisbury – they had been our neighbours when we retired. They had a lovely house and garden and a thatched barn next door. They took us to Montacute House, a National Trust property in Somerset.

When we eventually left them, we drove through the New Forest to Romsey and Mottisfont Abbey where the famous Rose Gardens were at their very best. We returned to the coast and found a B&B near Poole from where we visited Kingston Lacey and Compton Acres (gardens) and finally Brownsea Island which has a special place in my heart. It was Dick's first visit and he loved the Nature Reserve. We then travelled along the coast to Sussex to have a few days with Barbara, lunch with Rosemary and Pete at Steyning and a visit to Dorothy Rudd, widow of one of Dick's army officers who we used to see regularly on our earlier holidays at Bognor Regis.

The usual round of grandchildren, gardening and fruit preserving saw out the summer and by October we had itchy feet again. Our friends Jean and Frank invited us to join them on a trip to the Moselle Valley in Germany. Frank drove through the night and we arrived in Cochem about 10:30am rather weary and all ready for a 'Kaffee und Kuchen'. We stayed in a lovely house on a hill overlooking the river where enormous hotel boats silently slipped by. In a neighbouring village, marks on the wall of a house showed us that the river had flooded to great heights over a number of years. One of the more recent floods was in December 1993 when the water rose above the downstairs windows. The highest showed that in February 1784 it reached halfway up the upstairs windows!

Other villages provided hotels and pubs for some wonderful evening meals. Cochem was a lovely town where we took a ride up the Sesselbahn (cable car) to see the view over the valley, with a cup of coffee. Bernkastel-Kues was most attractive with its half-timbered houses and shops. Here Frank insisted we sampled the Zwiebelkuchen for lunch. We were not disappointed. We visited the lovely town of Bacharach and took the ferry from Bingen to Rudesheim, and walked up the famous Drosselgasse with its numerous cafés and busking musicians. It was all very colourful.

It being October farmers everywhere were busy harvesting their grapes. Needless to say, we sampled a variety of different wines and brought home a car boot full!

Since the early 1950s Dick and his army comrades had been meeting in Manchester every November for a dinner and a lot of reminiscing. Inevitably, over the years, numbers had diminished though boosted for some time by wives and sometimes offspring. As we neared the Millennium it became obvious that this annual event would have to come to an end. So this year of 1998 sadly became the last 'muster'. I had marvelled at their commitment, comradeship and memories every time we met. People often asked me why they wanted to remember the war. How could they ever forget it? How could they forget the comrades they fought alongside and also of course the ones, their friends, who never came home. They had cemented a lasting bond between them.

Our year ended with another reunion of a quite different type. Dick and I had met at a Young Farmer's Club in the 1950s and we had kept in touch with a lot of our farmer friends. So we decided to organise a dinner in Nottingham for those we were able to contact. We met up with friends who we saw regularly, often at farmers' dances, and some whom we hadn't seen for many years. It was a great evening and there were some hilarious and humorous reminiscences being exchanged.

I have only mentioned dancing briefly but, in fact, it ran like a thread through most of our married life. Following that first evening at the Saracen's Head in Southwell there were numerous YFC dances, often in different village halls, many Farmers' Balls during the winter months where evening dress was the 'order of the day', and frequent dances in our new village hall. For many years the ladies wore floor length dresses until the 'New Look' took over in the 1970s.

Chapter 31

FIVE WEEKS CAMPING IN FRANCE (1999)

The last year of the century arrived, and so 1999 kicked off with a visit to Belper in Derbyshire to the museum at the hosiery factory once owned by the Brettle family. We were shown round by a former employee who showed us stockings similar to the ones made for Queen Victoria, and the black stockings worn by men after the death of Prince Albert in 1861. We discovered that in 1803 the business was owned by Ward, Brettle & Ward and shortly afterwards by George Brettle & Co. By 1830 it was the largest hosiery wholesaler in London and two years later the Princess Victoria had visited Belper as a young girl. Apparently earlier archives had been lost in the London blitz in the 1940s.

Our main summer holiday was another visit to France, first to stay with Jean and Monique. We met up with their family and grandchildren at the family farm which Monique's brother owns and runs. We were also taken on a day's tour of the Pays d'Auge region, notably the picturesque villages of Beuvron and Pont L'Éveque with their lovely timber-framed houses. Then we set off to camp in the Vendée region, basing ourselves at Les Biches, near Saint-Hilaire-de-Riez and discovering fresh territory at Saint-Gilles-Croix-de-Vie and Les Sables-d'Olonne. By chance we came across the lovely Parc Floral de la Court d'Aron at Saint-Cyr-en-Talmondais with its acres and acres of water-lily beds, as well as colourful gardens, and then we visited the lake at Apremont where David now has a caravan. On our way back to the ferry at St. Malo we spent a couple of nights at Dol-de-Bretagne which has an excellent campsite with numerous good facilities. At the Saturday morning market in Dol, I was fascinated by a colourful cockerel strutting about the streets prior to being sold dead or alive! We crossed the Channel overnight and spent the next two days catching up with family and friends on the south coast before heading home.

After almost five weeks away the garden was in great need of attention and we picked raspberries every day for a week. My brother Harry had been ill with cancer for some time and was now sadly much worse. We visited him in Nottingham every other day until he died towards the end of August.

In September we had a five-day coach trip to Devon, a county we had never really explored, staying in Bideford and visiting Barnstaple, Ilfracombe, Dunster, Lynton and Lynmouth, where we saw the museum depicting the terrible flood disaster of 1952 and also the floods a few years previously. Porlock Weir was lovely as was the picturesque village at Clovelly where we walked down the steep cobbled hill to the tiny harbour.

In October we discovered Highland Heritage, a Scottish coach company who owned several hotels in western Scotland and would pick us up in Mansfield. This time we were based in Dalmally for a week and did a thorough tour of the area, visiting half a dozen different towns and villages each day stopping for coffee, lunch and afternoon tea, with time to explore. The drive through Glencoe and over Rannoch Moor brought back memories of a day back in 1950, when we had struggled with a head wind and heavy rain on our bikes along this road. It was an excellent holiday with a lovely hotel and we used this company several more times.

There was much work to be done before the end of the year. In November some windows in the house were replaced and all the external woodwork painted. Then in December central heating was installed and the house was in chaos. It was only just up and running by Christmas. My diary tells me that I scrubbed the kitchen floor at 11pm on Christmas Eve after I'd been to the church Carol Service! It was our turn to host the New Year's Eve dinner party so there was more preparation to be done. Madge came to stay as usual and our friends Jean and Frank were here too. As the new Millennium arrived we watched numerous local fireworks and sent up our own rocket to mark the occasion. We then all played Rummikub until 3:30 am!

Chapter 32

ITALY, BLACK FOREST, FLOODS & FLOORS (2000)

Sunshine welcomed the new Millennium so we took ourselves off to Clumber Park for an exhilarating walk round the lake. As is customary on New Year's Day there was a cricket match in progress! We then took our New Year greetings to all three branches of the family before Madge went home. Back into a routine I had a spate of farm surveys to do for market research, and we both assembled some more flooring panels for David who was supplying them for large house projects in London. There were a few day trips to Derbyshire and we made our annual pilgrimage to Hodsock Priory to see their wonderful display of snowdrops.

By May it was time to think of holidays again, so we flew to Italy with our friends Mick and Sylvia as none of us had been before. We picked up our tour coach in Venice and made our first stopover at Riva del Garda. We then travelled on through Milan to Lake Maggiore for three nights. From here we were taken to Zermatt in Switzerland over the Simplon Pass for a day's sightseeing. The next day we had a boat trip to the Borrowmean Islands, first to the Isola Bella to visit the Palace Gardens and then to the island of Pescatori which was very pretty. We spent a day in Lugano where we were shown around a chocolate factory and came away with lots of goodies. Our next stopover was at Cadenabbia on Lake Como from where we visited Bellagio by ferry, exploring the town and the gardens at Villa Melzi. Another ferry took us to Tremezzo and the famous Villa Carlotta. Our hotel was big and pleasant with an excellent cuisine but there had been a mix up over the bedrooms. We finished up in a very small room at the back of the hotel when we had expected a lake view. While we were packing our case to leave, we found a lizard on the bed which very nearly ended up in our suitcase.

Our courier was rather disobliging so we were a bit upset as this was our 45th wedding anniversary. But the day turned out to be the highlight of the holiday as we set off for Verona and Venice. In Verona we were shown the Arena, Juliette's balcony and the market, before continuing to Venice where we had time to see most of the well-known sights and had a ride on a gondola. At the Murano glass factory Dick bought me a lovely blue necklace as an anniversary present. For our optional second week we had chosen a hotel beside Lake Garda not far from the town of Malcesine. It was an excellent hotel in every way with a garden full of olive trees for shade and a swimming pool. Across the road was a small beach beside the lake which we appeared to have to ourselves. As we had no transport this week, we took the ferry to a number of pretty villages such as Limone, Gargano and Gardone where we visited a stunning alpine garden. Another day we took the cable car up Monte Baldo with its lovely views and masses of wild flowers. At the end of the week our coach picked us up and took us to Venice for the flight home.

Back home there had been a lot of rain so the garden needed attention as did a mass of soft fruits. Grandchildren were clamouring to be taken swimming and for days out with picnics, including the new Farm Park near Edwinstowe which was a great hit. There were lots of fresh peas in the garden and I recorded having picked and shelled a 'bucket full' on three occasions. Then it was the turn of the runner beans with similar results. It certainly was a very productive vegetable patch!

In mid-August we collected Beryl from Oxford to spend two weeks with us and enjoyed lots of outings and shopping sprees. When the grandchildren were back at school we decided on a coach holiday to the Black Forest in Germany. We followed the Rhine to a hotel at Schomberg, stopping off at Boppard en route. There were visits to Baden-Baden with its lovely Casino

Gardens, and to Freudenstadt where numerous fountains squirt intermittently from between the paving slabs in the square, providing entertainment for young and old alike. The shops were particularly attractive and it was here that I bought the loveliest jacket I have ever owned. We travelled through the beautiful Schiltach Valley to the cuckoo clock shop at Gutach which we found really fascinating. In the café there we partook of the best apple strudel ever – straight from the oven. Back at the hotel an enormous Black Forest Gateau awaited us. It had truly been a day of treats!

We spent most of the next day in Triberg visiting the museum, the wonderful carving workshops and the famous Christmas Shop full of attractive toys. We then walked up the path beside the enormous waterfall and the coach picked us up at the top. Our last day was spent in Heidelberg again with lovely shops including the famous Kathy Wolfharts where I bought presents for the grandchildren and some very nice Christmas Tree decorations. On our way home via the Holiday Inn at Ghent, we visited the town of Ypres with its magnificent buildings and the wonderful Menin Gate with the names of soldiers who fell in the First World War. A stop-off at a chocolate factory completed our journey before crossing the English Channel home.

In November a group of six of us went on a five-day coach trip to the Cotswolds staying at the Kings Arms in Cirencester. There had been a lot of heavy rain causing severe flooding in places. We spent a morning in the market towns of Moreton-in-Marsh and Stow-on-the-Wold, ending up having lunch in the attractive village of Bourton-on-the-Water and then later on to Bibury for a cup of tea. We weren't able to go to Worcester the next day because of flood water, so we drove through Gatcombe Park, the home of Princess Anne and next to Highgrove where Prince Charles lives. The small town of Tetbury provided us with coffee and some nice shops. Later we looked round Cirencester Abbey and Gardens. By now we had news of flooding at home, and were a little concerned at the speed at which water levels were rising in various parts of the country. We saw on television our beloved Meonstoke in Hants with roads impassable and, on our way to Tewkesbury, we spotted a herd of cattle stranded on a hillock at a farm which had also been shown on TV. In Tewkesbury the river was extremely high and several side roads were inundated, people's carpets and possessions had been thrown out on to the street due to the flooding of properties. The Abbey was completely surrounded by water. Gloucester was not much better but we did manage to visit the big Waterways Museum and the Cathedral.

The year ended with more rain, flooding and high winds.

During this year we had been assisting David with a joinery job. He was manufacturing floors for a work colleague for some prestigious London properties. We had the rather tedious task of putting together oak Versailles panels and small pieces of mosaic borders of many different timber species. It was very time consuming and he roped in Dick and I to help out.

We sat in his workshop fitting the tiny pieces of timber into a given pattern 3 inches wide and in one-yard lengths. They were then transported to London in batches. A lot of them were for large houses in Knightsbridge but, later on, work also went into the Art Gallery at Buckingham Palace.

Chapter 33

BACK TO 'LES POTS' & 9/11 ON TRIP TO AUSTRIA (2001)

The New Year of 2001 brought some much-needed sunshine so we went for our usual walk in Clumber Park. This was followed by a heavy hoar frost making the trees and the whole countryside very picturesque.

In April we went off to Hampshire, doing the rounds of friends and family and staying with the Lutyens' for three nights. A day was spent in the Queen Elizabeth Country Park which has lovely walks on the Downs and we picnicked by the village pond at Buriton. This village was a real find and we later stayed in a lovely thatched cottage there on more than one occasion. We found Dick's school friends Ted and Eileen at home in Meonstoke and spent some time reminiscing with them over coffee. On our way home we stayed with Beryl at Oxford for a couple of nights.

Back home, Easter was upon us and we found that Sophie, Lucy and Emily had booked themselves in! So more swimming and visits to Sherwood Forest seemed to be the order of the day, plus Grace's first birthday party at Barnstone. Lots more gardening to be done and it was time to plan our next holiday – another visit to Tony and Sharon's lovely house in France for two weeks, this time with our friends Jean and Frank, in their car.

At Portsmouth our ferry to Caen had been cancelled due to strike action, but we were transferred to another one on the route to St. Malo with a free cabin and some money towards petrol.

We broke our journey south at Niort for a night and then carried on to the house at Cercoux. This is a medium-sized village in the Charente-Maritime region a few kilometres inland from Bordeaux, with a small supermarket, two pâtisseries, garage and all amenities such as tennis courts etc. We were some way from the village, but there were bicycles in the outhouse (le chai) for some energetic person to fetch the croissants for breakfast. Most of our food shopping was done in the small attractive market town of Coutras, only a short drive away. Almost every day we had breakfast in the garden and lunch on the lawn under a gazebo as it was very hot. We had to keep our distance from one of the doors, as a pair of bluetits had a brood of chicks in a nest in the letter box and they seemed quite cross at our presence. In the evenings we had barbeques and the odd meal out. The surrounding area was fairly well explored and we spent a day at St. Emilion (well known for its wine) – another attractive and interesting place. We returned to Cercoux through acres and acres of vineyards.

It had been a relaxing holiday as the weather was so hot, but back home it was much cooler and we were able to catch up in the garden.

June, July and August were very busy with family and friends, gardening, and freezing masses of fruit and vegetables, but we managed a short break in Scotland staying at the Loch Achray Hotel. From here we visited the Royal Yacht Britannia moored at Leith which we found most enjoyable. This was followed by a coach tour of Edinburgh with frequent stops to explore. Caithness Glass near Perth was also on the itinerary as was a visit to Glamis Castle, home in the summer of the Queen Mother. Her gardens were immaculate and very colourful.

Towards the end of August we collected Beryl from Oxford for ten days and took her out and about, including a day in Derbyshire.

On the 11th September (9/11 as it became known) we set off on a coach trip to Austria. Part way down the A1 we received the news on the radio of the terrorist attack in New York. Overnight in Liege our TV showed us some other countries preparing for war – we wondered just how serious this was becoming, but the coach carried on and arrived at our hotel in Kirchdorf the next evening. The hotel had a nuclear shelter built into the mountainside and this was now a fantastic sports centre with numerous facilities. We used the swimming pool most days and had several games of snooker and table tennis. We left the fitness apparatus to the younger element!

Our first outing was to the lovely town of Kitzbuhel where we rode up the mountain in a cable car with magnificent views from the top. Another day we visited the spectacular Krimml Waterfalls in a minibus which took us through some stunning scenery. At the café near the falls we ate more delicious apple strudel with our companions from the coach, and discovered that two of them were Irish. They were quite upset to be told that we'd never been to Ireland and we felt a little ashamed, so we promised to go the following year, which we did! The next day we visited Alpbach, Pertisau, Achensee, Rattenberg and the Kisslinger glass shop, full of tempting jewellery and glassware of all kinds. Another day was spent sightseeing in Innsbruck with a guide and included the famous Golden Roof. On our final day we toured the Tyrol, again with magnificent scenery, stopping at Zell am See, Westendorf and Kirchberg.

We returned home to find that the threat of imminent war had diminished but the USA was in turmoil, with New York in crisis and many people dead. The autumn was mild and pleasant with temperatures in the 70s (Fahrenheit) some days. We went to Chatsworth one day to look for the seat which the Walker family had donated in memory of my cousin Joan. We couldn't find it but we did when we returned a week later. Joan had been evacuated to Chatsworth during the war from her boarding school in North Wales. She loved to play tennis so the seat had been sited near to where the tennis courts would have been. It is now the cut flower garden. We paid another visit to this beautiful stately home in December to see the Christmas displays and decorations. They were fantastic and still keep their reputation almost twenty years later.

Our year ended with a five-day coach trip to Bournemouth – new territory for us. We toured the resort and its neighbour Poole with a guide and had time to explore Poole Pottery. We also enjoyed the market at Ringwood, returning to our hotel through the New Forest with a stop at Burley for wine tasting. Our final outing was to Weymouth via Tolpuddle and Puddletown for shopping and on our journey home we passed a couple of hours in Winchester.

Chapter 34

FIRST OF MANY (26) VISITS TO MILFORD-on-SEA (2002)

When 2002 arrived the weather was mixed, so on wet or foggy days we got on with some decorating. On sunny days we managed a long walk at Clumber Park and a visit to Hodsock Priory snowdrops and, as ever, the grandchildren took over half-term week.

In March we set off for Hove to celebrate Auntie Freddie's 90th birthday, and en route we picked up Beryl from Oxford to take her to Rosemary and Pete's at Steyning, where we joined them later for two nights. While there we visited the village of Alfriston where the 14th century Clergy House was the first property to be acquired by the National Trust in 1896, for the sum of £10. It is a pretty thatched cottage with a small garden packed with flowers and vegetables. We had lunch at the Singing Kettle Tea House in Alfriston.

Later we walked round the lake at Sheffield Park (nowhere near Sheffield) which was very colourful with spring flowers, trees and shrubs.

On our return to Kidlington with Beryl we called at West Dean Gardens near Chichester which also displayed a mass of spring flowers. I was intrigued by the fruit trees there, as not only were there cordon, fan-trained and espalier trees but others trained into unusual shapes. I remember thinking how I would have loved to have worked in a garden like this. We stayed with Beryl for two nights and took her to some of the pretty Cotswold villages where Barbara and I had toured on our bikes more than 50 years before.

After leaving Beryl's we called in at Waddesdon Manor in Buckinghamshire – built by the eminent Rothschild family in 1874 in the style of a French château. Here the gardens are more formal but very colourful and the house has some real treasures not to be missed.

David and Sarah had earlier bought a holiday caravan at Milford-on-Sea near Lymington so we set off in April to spend our first of many holidays there. We found the tiny harbour at Keyhaven from where we could take the small ferry to Hurst Castle, built by Henry VIII to protect the Solent from the French. The castle can also be reached on foot via a one-and-a-half-mile shingle spit. We also visited Buckler's Hard situated on the Beaulieu River further along the coast. Here Henry VIII built his warship Agamemnon with oak cut from the New Forest nearby. There is a comprehensive Maritime Museum and a family hotel with lawns stretching down to the river, where barbeques can be enjoyed and boat trips run up and down the river.

Another day we drove west along the coast to Mudeford which stands on Christchurch Harbour at the mouth of the River Avon. We went into the Avonmouth Hotel for coffee and it was so pleasant and welcoming that we stayed for lunch too. In the years since then we have frequented the hotel for refreshment on numerous occasions. We have also stayed overnight in more recent years. Across the harbour is Mudeford Quay with some picturesque buildings, small fishing boats and stacks of lobster pots. A ferry takes you on a five-minute crossing to Mudeford Spit where there are a number of very colourful beach huts – all extremely expensive. There is a very pleasant sandy beach but in bad weather it is somewhat exposed. A miniature railway will take you a mile or so to a café near the large car park which is approachable from the Bournemouth area. There are also lots of footpaths up and over Hengistbury Head. This location has turned out to be a much-frequented area by the rest of our family.

Some of the gardens which we like to re-visit are Spinners, near Lymington and the vast expanse of Exbury Gardens across the river from Buckler's Hard. These are spectacular in spring with rhododendrons and azaleas, and are worth a return visit in October just to see the autumn colours. There is of course the whole of the New Forest to explore which is steeped in history. The villages of Brockenhurst and Burley are inviting, the towns of Lyndhurst and Lymington are packed with good quality shops and eateries, the latter sporting an extensive Saturday market that runs the entire length of the High Street.

From Lepe Park and Calshott Point the Isle of Wight is clearly visible and we have watched the annual 'Round the Island' yacht race from there. It is also interesting to see the huge container ships and cruise ships going in and out of Southampton Water from the vantage points. As they turn to enter the narrow passage they are so overpowering and come so close to the shore, they make you want to turn and run! There is so much to see and do in that area that we stayed in David and Sarah's caravan more than a dozen times, and when they sold it we found a small site nearby and stayed there twelve more times, often going three times a year.

In June we were off to France again on a camping holiday. This time we chose to cross to St. Malo and spent a day exploring the Emerald Coast, before staying the night in Dinan which is a town we found very attractive and returned there on several occasions. We drove south along the Atlantic Coast to our campsite at Les Amiaux near Saint-Jean-de-Monts.

We had a relaxing holiday with plenty of swimming in both sea and pool and picnic lunches in the lovely pine forests that line the coast. A selection of restaurants provided evening meals. We spent a day in the attractive town of Pornic which became a favourite of ours. We also paid a visit to the perfumed botanical gardens at Coex which were something quite different. Before returning home we had three days with Jean and Monique at Cahagnes, and once back in England broke our journey at Beryl's for a night.

In August we fetched Beryl to stay with us for ten days and spent a lot of the time with the family.

Tony and Sharon celebrated their Silver Wedding in September with an excellent Sunday lunch at Palace House in Newmarket, followed by tea in the garden at their lovely Newmarket home. We stayed in a very good bed & breakfast and, before coming home, we had a look at Wicken Fen and Anglesey Abbey (both National Trust properties) the gardens of the latter being ablaze with colour.

During the October half-term we entertained the grandchildren with the usual round of swimming and outings plus a visit to the Palace Theatre in Newark to see Emily dancing with her dance class. It was an excellent performance.

Soon after, Madge came to stay and we took advantage of the mild weather, spending a couple of days in Derbyshire where the autumn colours were at their best.

In mid-November we sampled a 'Turkey and Tinsel' five-day coach break in North Wales, staying in Criccieth and visiting Anglesey, Portmadoc and the Ffestiniog Railway, plus a tour of some popular spots like Bettys-y-Coed and Pwelhi on market day.

Chapter 35

A NIGHT IN DICK'S CHILDHOOD BEDROOM & CARAVANNING TAKES OVER (2003)

The New Year of 2003 began very cold and there were floods at Fiskerton and Kelham making the roads impassable. There was a lot of snow in places blocking roads, but not ours in Rolleston.

When March arrived the weather tempted us to make our first foray south. We explored Warwick and the Castle, staying at a farm with a luxurious feather bed. It had been years since I had slept in one. We passed through a number of our favourite Cotswold villages and had two nights with Beryl at Oxford, before heading for Worthing and a few days with Barbara and Reg.

While there we had lunch with Auntie Freddie at Hove. Before leaving Sussex we just had to call at Bognor Regis and Bosham, before heading on to Meonstoke where we had booked into Periwinkle Cottage which is now a bed & breakfast and was the actual house where Dick lived as a boy. We even slept in his old bedroom and, of course, out came all the reminiscences! We again caught up with some of his old school friends before heading home.

Alas! While we had been away enjoying ourselves, the mice had also had a party. They had eaten every one of the 140 broad bean seeds I had sown in the greenhouse!

On April 2nd, Madge's birthday, we took her to Derbyshire and had lunch at one of our favourite hotels – the Sir William at Grindleford and then tea at Chatsworth where the Camellias were in full bloom.

At the end of April we set off for the caravan at Milford-on-Sea for the second time, staying overnight at a lovely B&B in the Chiltern Hills. This became a regular stopover on our way south. From here we planned our route through some pretty villages in the Thames Valley, almost always stopping at a delightful coffee shop in Kingsclere. Soon after this we joined the valley of the River Test where we encountered more picturesque villages.

At Longparish we counted over twenty thatched cottages. Wherwell is spectacular with a much-photographed cottage completely covered in roses in June. At Fullerton a road is lined with about half a mile of cherry blossom trees in May and then comes the adorable little town of Stockbridge. Our lunch stop was usually a picnic on the grassy car park at Mottisfont Abbey with its lovely gardens. Alternatively, not far away was the Bear and Ragged Staff which would supply our needs if it rained. At Romsey we entered the New Forest, a delight at any time of the year, passing through Lyndhurst and Lymington on our way to the coast. While there we visited the usual favourite spots like Keyhaven, near where we discovered Braxton Gardens which became a regular haunt for coffee and lunch. The 'olde worlde' Gun at Keyhaven also became a much-frequented hostelry. We returned to Mudeford Quay and the Avonmouth Hotel for refreshment, and while exploring the New Forest we came across the Owl and Otter Sanctuary at Ashurst which was very interesting to us. Our friends Rosalind and Sandy who live in the New Forest came to have tea with us at the caravan and invited us back to their home in Sway, which remained a regular port of call whenever we were in the area.

The month ended with two parties on one day. Chesterfield was the venue for our friends David and Marion's Golden Wedding, which was held in their garden on a lovely warm day with all their family. It was also Dick's cousin Ruth and husband Victor's Ruby Wedding Day and luckily their party was in the evening, also held in the garden with a large number of family and friends, many of the ladies in beautiful West African dress.

At the beginning of July Sarah phoned to say they couldn't go to Centre Parcs at Elveden as planned as Sophie had chickenpox, and invited us to take up the booking. So we packed hurriedly and off we went. We explored the site, played snooker, swam in the tropical pool and sampled a variety of eateries in the evenings. On our way home we stayed a night in Ely and called on Tony and Sharon at Newmarket for lunch.

The following week we had lunch with Mick and Sylvia at Sutton-on-Trent and sat in the garden all afternoon on their new swing hammock. Sylvia was excited at the prospect of taking a coach trip to Eastern Europe the following week. Sadly it was the last time we were to see her, as she died in Poland on that holiday following many years of heart problems. We had lost a very good friend from our farming days - with whom we had shared many enjoyable holidays in retirement.

The end of July and beginning of August were very hot, the thermometer registering over 30 degrees C on two days. After we had watched England win the Test Match by 53 runs, we set off to spend a week with Beryl. We found some more pretty villages in the Cotswolds and the Chilterns as yet unexplored by us, where we had picnic lunches as the weather was perfect. While we were having tea at the Bull and Butcher at Turville the waitress told us about the filming of Chitty, Chitty, Bang, Bang in the village, and pointed to the windmill up the hill that had appeared in the film.

Barbara made a brief visit to us for a weekend and we took her to Chatsworth and some local garden centres as she is a keen gardener herself, forever on the lookout for something new for her garden.

Then we were off on another coach holiday to Scotland, a ten-hour journey to Loch Tummel and a new area waiting to be explored. Days out included visits to Blair Castle, Pitlochry, Dunkeld and Aviemore where we rode on the

Strathspey Steam Railway. We then went to the Top of Cairngorm on the funicular railway from where we had wonderful views as the weather was very clear. Another day we travelled to Royal Deeside via Glen Shea where the autumn colours were absolutely stunning. Our final outing was to the Caithness Glass factory near Perth and a lavender centre for shopping, finishing up in St. Andrews.

Our autumn visit to the caravan at Milford-on-Sea covered two weeks, with a break in the middle to visit Rosemary and Pete in Sussex and have lunch with Auntie Freddie. Back at the caravan David had arrived with Sophie, Lucy and Emily for part of the half-term. We all spent time crabbing from the little bridge near Keyhaven, a favourite spot for all the family, and of course a visit to Wootton Bridge in the New Forest where the girls explored and climbed trees overhanging the river and where we would usually take a picnic. We always tried to pay a visit to Smugglers Cove at the end of a long, narrow lane and quite isolated where we believe smugglers used to bring ashore their contraband. It was always very muddy with rock pools and had a strange air about it, but the girls loved it. We rarely saw anyone else there as there was nowhere to park other than on the shingle beach.

When the family had returned home, we visited Exbury Gardens to see the autumn colours and discovered Furzey Gardens which were smaller but equally beautiful. We also spent a day at Christchurch, returning to enjoy the Priory which we had first visited almost 50 years ago, and of course finished the day with a meal at the Avonmouth Hotel. That was our sixth holiday of the year!

We returned home to prepare for Christmas and the New Year when as usual Madge was coming to stay for a week.

Chapter 36

60th ANNIVERSARY OF D-DAY IN NORMANDY (2004)

Over the New Year of 2004 we discussed plans to try a 'Winter Warmer' short break provided by some of the coach companies. We settled on Whitby towards the end of January accompanied by our friends Jean and Frank. Our accommodation was at the excellent Royal Hotel on the cliff top looking out to sea. We were taken to Durham for a day – a lovely city and as yet not visited by us – and spent a long time in the beautiful cathedral. Another day we toured the North Yorkshire Moors, passing the pointed hill named Roseberry Topping and nicknamed the 'Yorkshire Matterhorn'. There was still plenty of time to explore Whitby on foot.

We were now getting itchy feet again, so at the end of February we went to Scotland by coach staying in Dalmally again. My plan had been to get some really wintery photographs but we found only the slightest dusting of snow on the highest peaks. However, it was extremely cold and frosty so that the water at the edge of some of the Lochs was frozen, as were most of the waterfalls. We had a tour of the Famous Grouse whisky distillery at Crieff, the lovely port of Oban, Seil Island and Stirling Castle. We even braved a chilly boat trip on Loch Lomond.

In April Barbara and Reg invited us to Worthing for Easter. They took us to West Dean Gardens again which were ablaze with spring flowers, and then on to Highdown which is a delightful garden set on a hill. The chalk soil of the South Downs produces wonderful displays of many flowers we cannot grow successfully at home in Nottinghamshire. From Worthing we went to the caravan at Milford where David and the girls were visiting for a few days. The highlight of the week was a visit to an Alpine Centre where the girls spent the afternoon on ski bobs and rings. They had a great time on the slippery slopes.

In June we were off to Normandy to celebrate the 60th anniversary of D-Day, but first we had a week in a caravan at Saint-Gilda-de-Rhuys on the Morbihan Peninsular. It was extremely hot so we didn't venture very far. The site and the surrounding area were not as appealing as previous campsites in the Vendée region. However, we did explore a bit and had a good rest before joining Jean and Monique at Cahagnes for the re-union weekend. There was the usual service at the memorial, followed by a superb banquet at the château in the centre of Flers. This was then followed by the presentation of a medal to every one of the veterans. Our last day with Jean and Monique was spent lunching by the river in the Suisse Normande and a return visit to the fantastic model railway museum at Clecy.

Back home, and July was given over to entertaining grandchildren, gardening and preserving fruit and vegetables. We spent Dick's birthday in Derbyshire, taking Madge with us and walking in Millers Dale.

The following weekend Rosemary and Pete came to stay and joined us for the usual family barbeque. August began with a heat wave, and then the weather broke and we had heavy rain and thunderstorms for the rest of the month. The grandchildren rummaged through the dressing-up box and played endless board games. We did manage some trips to the swimming pool though. When they had gone home Madge came to stay for a week, and summer returned in September enabling us to have some enjoyable days out. At the end of the month, we went off to the caravan at Milford for two weeks plus a couple of nights with Barbara at Worthing.

The last week in October we had four days on a Scottish coach trip with our retired farming friends Bob and Beryl, staying on the side of Loch Lomond at the Inversnaid Hotel. As well as coach outings to Inverary, Oban and Glencoe we were treated to a ride on the Falkirk Wheel – a massive piece of engineering which will carry boatloads of passengers from one level of water to another, without the need for a lock. It was a memorable, exhilarating experience.

On Remembrance Sunday in November Sophie and Lucy paraded with the Guides and Brownies at Farnsfield. Dick was invited to march with the Royal British Legion old comrades there. He dutifully joined them, also marching the following two years while the girls were involved.

Our December calendar was full of school concerts and Christmas plays, the likes of which we attended over several years. We spent Christmas Day at David and Sarah's and on Boxing Day the whole family of fifteen came to us for lunch. This had become an annual event and so too had the arrival of Madge for the New Year.

Chapter 37

OUR GOLDEN YEAR (2005)

Here we are in 2005 and this is our 'Golden Year'.

We shall have been married for fifty years on May the 19th. We get wind of the boys planning something more than a party. But first we had to face winter and early spring. However, it turned out to be reasonably mild with some sun and only one heavy fall of snow in February.

So in January we took another 4-day 'Winter Warmer' coach break with Jean and Frank to Weston-Super-Mare. While there we had a lovely day in Bath visiting the Abbey and the Roman Baths, having afternoon tea in the famous Pump Room with the orchestra playing some of the old tunes. It was all very Victorian and I felt we should have been wearing long dresses and hats and carrying a parasol. We had a long walk in Weston-Super-Mare and found the Jill Dando memorial garden. She had been a well-loved TV presenter who had been murdered on her doorstep in 1999.

At the beginning of March Jean and Monique's eldest son Stephane brought his wife Nathalie and children Caroline and Augustin to stay with David, and I joined them to act as interpreter! We took them into Sherwood Forest to see the Major Oak as the children wanted to know where Robin Hood lived, and then to Rufford Abbey with its extensive parkland and lake. Another day we took them swimming and to shop in Newark. They left us to spend two days sightseeing in London.

Auntie Freddie celebrated her 93rd birthday in March. As she had been ill in hospital, we decided to go down to Sussex to visit her. We stayed with Barbara who took us to another new garden, Denmans, which is well worth a visit, and to the RSPB Centre at Pulborough Brooks for a spot of bird watching. On our return journey we spent a day with Beryl at Oxford.

Soon after this we had a visit from our French friends Jean and Monique. It was hard work trying to emulate the superior cuisine of Monique, doing all the translating and the driving when we took them about, but we all enjoyed ourselves. When they left at the end of the month we packed the car and went off to David's caravan for a rest. Dick hadn't driven since he had polymyalgia in 1997, but as I had always loved driving all was well.

In May Luke celebrated his 18th birthday with a dinner party at Damons near Lincoln. How the years had flown. It didn't seem five minutes since he was half that age and we were entertaining him and Matthew regularly and taking them on holiday.

On May 19th we celebrated our big day with lunch at the Sir William at Grindleford in Derbyshire – one of our favourite eateries. We took along our friends Jean and Frank, and Madge who had been my bridesmaid, and we also met up with David and Marion from Chesterfield. It was a lovely sunny day and we had an excellent lunch, followed by a very pleasant walk.

At the end of the month came the big surprise. The boys had booked a farmhouse in the Vendée region of France for a week for nine of us.

Unfortunately, Peter and family were unable to go. We took the overnight ferry to Ouistreham and drove down with David and the girls, with Eddie and family following, to La Grande Barbiere near Chantonnay. The farmhouse was huge so we were able to spread out. David chose the ground floor bedroom with a sink in the corner. One day he was greeted by a grass snake which had come out from under the sink. He didn't let it worry him – just made sure nothing was left on the floor, especially at night. There was a good-sized swimming pool in the garden which we used every day as the weather was extremely hot. Jacob, who was six, took his first swimming strokes without his inflatable ring that week. We put Caroline in charge of catering and she came up with some delicious French cuisine. Naturally we all helped with the preparation, cooking and washing up and we included some barbecues in the large back garden. We went out to a lakeside restaurant on Emily's 13th birthday and found other good dinner venues as well.

Our outings were to La Tranche-sur-Mer and Les Sable-d'Olonne to spend time on the beach, and to the little market town of Les Herbiers which had some nice shops. On our return journey from the holiday we called on Jean and Monique and had a meal with them and Stephane and family, who had come 200 miles from Paris to see us.

The garden took over in June and July along with school sports days and then we fetched Madge for two weeks while the grandchildren were away on holiday. Dick had never been a theatre-goer but he liked the music of Abba, so near to his birthday we all took him to Nottingham Theatre Royal to see Abba Mania and he loved it. Madge accompanied us to Derbyshire and the Vale of Belvoir on days out, and happily helped me pick and freeze soft fruits. When she returned home, we were raring to go again.

This time we had a twelve-hour journey by coach to the north coast of Scotland staying at the Dornoch Hotel, which was excellent. The first day we toured the local area with some stunning scenery. The next day was the highlight of the week – a visit to Orkney. The crossing from John O'Groats was a little choppy which is not unusual, but we saw Scapa Flow and the Churchill Barriers.

After lunch in Kirkwall we had time to visit the shops and the cathedral, before being taken to see the standing stones at Skara Brae and the wonderfully ornate Italian Chapel, built by Italian prisoners of war in the 1940s. We were told that several of them had returned with their families to re-visit their elegant piece of craftsmanship. It was well worth the long journey to see it. Another day we toured the North West Highlands to Durness, driving along more than 30 miles of single-track roads, again the scenery was stunning. In the evening there was a pipe band parade in Dornoch with dancing in the street. There was also a visit to a whisky distillery, a winery for tasting, to Inverness and Ullapool, Strathpeffer and Dingwall, to the museum. We saw salmon leaping at Shin Falls and a very old church at Nigg, site of a hidden village buried in the sand. It was a very full week but we still had enough energy to walk on the beach and over the extensive golf course in the evenings.

We hadn't been home long when Barbara came to stay for a few days and then we heard that Auntie Freddie was back in hospital. So we drove to Sussex to see her, this time staying with Rosemary and Pete. We were glad we had gone, as she died ten days later. In just over a week we were back in Brighton for her funeral.

Instead of coming home we drove to the caravan as David and the girls were down there for half term. We frequented most of our favourite spots but it rained heavily for two days and was very windy, causing some very rough seas. We could hear the waves crashing all night long.

While shopping in Southwell one day in November, my eye was attracted to a large poster in the window of the travel agent. It was a photograph of several enormous waterfalls at Geiranger Fjord in Norway. I remarked to a couple standing beside me how wonderful it looked, "It is" they said, "we've been." The advertisement was for the Hurtigruten which is a coastal voyage between Bergen and the North Cape, and sets out daily throughout the year at 8pm from Bergen and takes 12 days there and back. There are a dozen or so of these ships which carry everything imaginable, including the daily post, from port to port along Norway's west coast. They take passengers too and the local people use them to visit relatives and go to business appointments. They also accommodate a large number of holiday passengers. I had heard of it before and was interested, having already made three visits to Norway and loved it.

As my aunt had just left me a generous legacy the holiday was do-able. I went in and picked up a brochure, hurried home and placed it on Dick's lap. He liked it! "Yes," he said, "if you're paying." So we booked for the following June to be there for the longest day when the sun doesn't sink below the horizon.

Chapter 38

THE HURTIGRUTEN (2006)

Our first outing in 2006 was a 'Winter Warmer' in Exmouth. We visited Sidmouth and Exeter, where we spent time in the beautiful cathedral with its lovely carvings. We also visited Teignmouth and Dawlish, home to the famous black swans. A boat trip on the River Exe completed our short break. Back at home I noted in my diary that we heard the woodpecker drumming continuously almost every day for three weeks in January. Then in April the cuckoo was heard most days. Sadly these two birds are rarely heard in this area nowadays.

We regularly took Madge and Marigold out for a pub lunch, often into our favourite Derbyshire, but also discovering a new venue at Widmerpool called the Pullman, which was a converted railway carriage, and they provided an excellent menu.

There was just time to pull in a week at the caravan before we began to pack for our great adventure on the Hurtigruten – our first and only cruise.

We flew to Bergen on June 11th on a small twin-prop plane carrying only 50 passengers. Our ship was MS Polarlys which left Bergen at 8pm. Our cabin was comfortable with a porthole. During the night I remember being aware that the engines were slowing and I looked out to see the lights of our first port of call. It was quite spectacular and I must say I was really excited. The first stop in daylight was at Ålesund where we watched hundreds of pallets of supplies being unloaded, along with bigger items. This was one of the shorter stops – about half an hour – where passengers were requested to stay on board. The stops varied in length up to about three hours, where trips ashore had been organised.

From Ålesund we sailed through the Romsdal region and to Geirangerfjord where we saw some of the highest and most magnificent waterfalls in the world. They were numerous and very impressive. There was an added bonus when Queen Sonja passed us in her launch and waved to us. Some of our passengers had chosen to disembark and take a coach ride over the mountains to Molde where we picked them up later in the day.

Our next lengthy stop was at Trondheim – the original capital of Norway. We had time to visit the very grand cathedral noted for its beautiful Rose Window and the Ringve Music Museum where different instruments were played for us in each room. Early in the morning of day four we crossed the Arctic Circle. There was a competition to guess the exact time of crossing and the winner had a bucket of ice poured down their neck! So did lots of passengers but we 'chickened out'.

Our next stop was Bodo – a centre for trade and communication and a very busy town. We disembarked and spent an hour or so watching the shipping activities at the port. The seemed to be ships of all shapes and sizes everywhere. From Bodo we crossed the open sea to the Lofoten Islands stopping briefly at Stamsund and Svolvær – the capital – with supplies. The islands are composed of fishing villages with fishermen's cabins built everywhere. Then we steamed back towards the mainland coast, where we disembarked at Tromsø to visit the Polar Museum and the magnificent modern cathedral. There are several very fine bridges in this area carrying more and more traffic to the many large offshore islands.

At last we arrived at the North Cape, passing towns and villages to be visited on our return journey. Honningsvåg is the capital of the North Cape with 3,500 inhabitants. From here we went by coach to visit a Sami settlement, complete with wigwams and sleighs and about 150,000 reindeer. The Sami people prefer not to be called Lapps these days.

Next stop was the North Cape with its magnificent globe monument standing on a bleak, windswept promontory, there we had plenty of time to take photos and tour the extensive museum. Disappointingly it was misty so we couldn't see far out into the Barents Sea, but it wasn't hard to imagine the island of Spitsbergen 500 miles away and then 800 miles beyond to the North Pole!

Back on-board ship we called at Mehamn and then waited for one of our sister ships, the MS Midnatsol, to leave the tiny harbour at Berlevåg before we could enter. It was 11pm and the sun was shining, so our favourite sister ship performed her traditional ritual of sending up balloons and waving pillow cases as we passed. Until 1970 the coastal voyage was unable to call at Berlevåg due to Arctic storms, and the inhabitants were often cut off from the outside world. But then a new sea wall was built using 15-tonne concrete tetrapods that bind together while allowing some water to flow through. I thought it made a rather attractive harbour.

The next day we arrived at Kirkenes where the ship turned round to retrace its voyage south. But first there was a visit by coach to the Russian border 9 miles away – not very exciting! Then we were taken to a disused iron ore mine to see a tunnel where 2,500 people sheltered for 2 months in 1944, before being liberated by the Russians. Ten babies were born in the tunnel.

We sailed between numerous islands off the north coast of Finnmark to Havøysund, passing tons and tons of fish hanging out to dry on pyramidal racks. Disembarking at Hammerfest, regarded as the world's most northerly town, we also discovered a vibrant Sunday market. The beautiful modern city was built after the original was razed to the ground by the Germans as they left in 1944. We were surprised to meet a coach-load of people from Lincoln who were travelling north. Later that evening we made a return visit to Tromsø, some of us disembarking to attend a midnight concert in the beautiful Arctic Cathedral built in 1965. When we emerged an hour later (1am) the sun was streaming across the water, lighting up the elegant modern bridge. It was one of those eureka moments!

The next morning we arrived back in the Lofoten Islands where we had some time in Svolvær. At the WW2 Museum we learned of the cruel treatment of the inhabitants and the many deaths from starvation. Later in the evening we passed through the narrow Raftsundet Strait with mountains towering on either side. The channel twists and turns along a 12-mile stretch and it seemed as if we should never get through. We entered the tiny Trollfjord just before midnight and I took a good photo without a flashgun! Modern ships can turn around in their own length which we did, as we were only taken there for the excitement. Back out at sea in the morning we were soon passing the Maelstrom, a significant whirlpool which can be fatal to small boats. Soon we were re-crossing the Arctic Circle and leaving behind the 'Land of the Midnight Sun'.

On day 10 we arrived back in Trondheim where a number of passengers disembarked to take the train to Oslo. But as we had already been there twice, we elected to spend our last two nights back in Bergen. That midnight (20th June) we watched as the sun sank to the horizon but never disappeared. It immediately began to rise, as this was now the longest day - another splendid moment on the voyage. As we approached Bergen, we were invited onto the bridge to meet the First Officer who spoke good English and told us the history of Hurtigruten AS, which began in 1893 with just two ships – there are now fourteen. We then watched him guide the ship into Brønnøysund, our last brief port of call.

Sadly we said goodbye to MS Polarlys – it had been a remarkable voyage, the ship providing every comfort and an outstanding cuisine. The scenery had been phenomenal!

Back in Bergen it was raining as usual. They say it rains approximately 280 days of the year and the inhabitants carry an umbrella even when the sun is shining! But we were not deterred and next morning set off on foot to explore the extensive fish and flower markets, the lovely coloured houses on the waterfront - Bryggen - and the old wooden houses similar to those once occupied by the Hanseatic Merchants in the 14th Century. We then joined a little road-train which gave us a thorough tour of the town and up over Mt. Floyen where we were able to walk in the woodland.

In the afternoon we were taken first to the wooden stave church at Fantoft which replaced the 12th century one which had burnt down in 1992. Luckily, detailed drawings had been kept of the original church and I hardly noticed any difference from the one I had visited in 1953. From there we went to Troldhaugen, the home of the composer Edvard Greig for 22 years. The house is furnished as it was in his day, his rimless glasses lying beside an open book, and his piano is still used for recitals. The little cabin where he worked still sits beside Lake Nordas at the bottom of the garden. Since my previous visit a small concert hall has been built and several of us returned that evening for a concert. That was a real bonus. We flew home the next morning.

That was the second of my 'holidays of a lifetime', comparing favourably with Switzerland in 1982. Both had the most wonderful mountain scenery, one having snow in abundance and the other 24-hour sunshine.

After our return home we experienced a very hot and dry July, followed by a much cooler and windy August. The highlight for me was to change the car and buy a second-hand Mercedes. I had never imagined myself driving one of these beauties, but it was the best and most comfortable car I ever owned and it took us everywhere for 12 years. However, we did sample rail travel for two days when we rode on the Carlisle-Settle line and the Severn Valley railway. In September we took a 5-day coach break in Belgium, staying in Antwerp, a lovely old town on the River Schelt where Dick's 11th Armoured Division had fought a fierce battle during the war. While there we visited the famous diamond factory and museum. Other towns we discovered that had been re-built with some impressive architecture were Ghent, Mechelen and Louvein, all with outstandingly beautiful cathedrals.

We had two weeks at the caravan in October when the autumn colours in the New Forest were at their best. The weather was fine and mild so we were able to go to all our favourite places, plus a visit to Uppark, a National Trust property which had burnt down and been re-built to its former glory. We were told a long chain of volunteers had removed pretty well all of the furniture and valuable contents while the fire was still raging.

In December we took our friends Doug and Olga to Chatsworth to see the Christmas Spectacular depicting the twelve days of Christmas, which was extremely well presented. To end the year David took us and his girls to Edale in Derbyshire for a walk up Mam Tor.

Chapter 39

DAVID'S CARAVAN PROVES A WINNER (2007)

Madge came for the New Year as usual but we didn't venture far as the weather was bad. By the middle of the month there were terrific gales and heavy rain throughout Britain, causing flooding in many places including Kelham Road. Trees and lorries were blown over and I lost my lovely Larch tree. Eleven people were killed.

At the end of the month we had a 'Winter Warmer' four-day break at Windermere with Jean and Frank, visiting Grasmere and Ambleside and spending some time in Keswick. We had pleasant spring weather at half-term making it easier to entertain the grandchildren. More good weather at Easter meant gardening could begin in earnest and so, with seeds sown and plants planted, we went off to the caravan as it was still very warm and sunny and stayed for two weeks. We discovered two new gardens well worth a visit – Spinners near Lymington and Hinton Ampner en route to Meonstoke.

In May we had the promised holiday in Ireland on a coach touring the Dingle Peninsular and the Ring of Kerry. I was very impressed with the scenery and we had several stops with time to explore, including the rose garden in Tralee, Blarney Castle and Bunratty Castle, with a ride in a pony and trap. We finished with a guided tour of Dublin.

At the beginning of June we visited Doddington Hall near Lincoln mainly to see their spectacular display of irises. A lot of these were finished but there were many beds of other flowers to enjoy. I had recently bought a mobility scooter and was able to get round the vast gardens on it. It was used frequently at that time when we took the grandchildren to Clumber Park, their favourite venue for games of hide and seek among the extensive plantings of rhododendrons. These outings usually ended with food at their favourite cafe The Old School House at Carburton. They will have happy memories of these occasions.

On 15th June Peter celebrated his 50th birthday with a big party and barbeque at Rolleston Village Hall. A week later he set off on his motorbike on a sponsored week-long tour in northern France to raise money for Clic Sergeant, a charity supporting children with cancer. A group of 26 took part and they raised a substantial amount of money. Unfortunately, it rained heavily every single day which ruined their potential enjoyment of the scenery. We had similar weather here causing floods in many local villages.

Most of July and August were taken up with grandchildren, but Dick was taken ill with pleurisy and spent a few days in hospital, which prevented us from going to Darren and Charlie's wedding at Chilham in Kent. We were very disappointed as the reception was being held in the castle in this very pretty village. However, my cousin Mary and Alan brought the photos to show us which we were able to project onto our TV screen.

After a lovely 80th birthday party for Ruth at Cotgrave the diary appeared to be empty, so we went off to the caravan again for 2 weeks. We did all the usual things and relaxed with a jigsaw puzzle and played a lot of Rummikub. While there we had visits from our friends Rosalind and Sandy who live in the New Forest, and Ro and Pete came over from West Sussex. One day we went to Hythe Waterfront opposite Southampton, had a ride on the old pier train and sat and watched the huge container ships coming up Southampton Water from the Solent.

We were home in time for Kate's birthday and then 3 days later the birth of Alfie Liam. Ten days at home was long enough to deal with the last of the beans and pears and, of course, enjoy our new grandson so we went back to the caravan for one last visit. We had to say our 'goodbye' to it as David was selling it. We had been there a dozen times. However, we found a small private site nearby and rented a caravan there for a further twelve visits. Needless to say, we love the area.

Christmas followed the usual pattern – we spent Christmas Day with David, and then on Boxing Day we had our family lunch at the Bromley Arms at Fiskerton followed by 14 for tea at Rolleston.

Chapter 40

LAST VISIT TO JEAN & MONIQUE IN NORMANDY (2008)

We began the New Year with a visit to the panto – Dick Whittington at Nottingham Playhouse – along with David and the girls.

There was a cold, wet, windy spell with more local flooding. A 'Winter Warmer' beckoned and we found it and plenty of sunshine on a 4-day break to Eastbourne. We visited Brighton and had lunch at the Dome, and then saw stacks and stacks of timber washed up onto the beach from a container ship that had run aground. We returned to the hotel via Beachy Head. The following day we were dropped off on the front at Hastings and had a long walk into town to explore. Each evening we witnessed murmurations of starlings as they alighted on the end of the pier which was visible from our hotel bedroom window. We also had a friendly seagull regularly tapping on our window.

In February David painted the kitchen and laid new floor tiles. The grandchildren were here for half term and it was very cold and frosty, -6, -7 and -8 degrees being recorded in my diary.

At 12:57 on 27th Feb there was an earthquake registering 5.2 on the Richter Scale. I was woken by what sounded like a train passing through the bedroom. Doors rattled and ornaments wobbled but no damage was done. We got up and put the television on to be told the epicentre was somewhere in Lincolnshire. There were some roof tiles dislodged in Newark.

On Easter Saturday we celebrated 50 years at Rolleston with a heavy fall of snow, but it soon disappeared.

At the beginning of May we had a week's coach holiday in Scotland staying at the Gairloch Hotel on the west coast. It was a lovely holiday with warm sunny weather. We visited the Inverewe Gardens Estate, somewhere I had had on my wish list, and were not disappointed. It was all very colourful with spring growth and flowers which had already bloomed at home. The wonderful display of camassias sent me straight off to buy some and they still gladden my heart year after year. There was still some time to explore Ullapool later that day. We spent the whole of the next day on the Isle of Skye where it was so hot, we had to seek shade from some trees. Another day we visited Inverness and the Moniak Winery for a tasting session, returning via Drumnadrochit and keeping an eye out for the 'Loch Ness Monster'! On our last full day we went by minibus through the Torridon Mountains to Applecross, a pretty little isolated village where we had lunch. It was a most enjoyable day as the road was narrow and twisty, and the scenery reminded me very much of Switzerland. Our journey home next day brought us through Pitlochry and the Trossachs and over the Erskine Bridge to Glasgow where we broke the journey home.

We were home in time for Luke's 21st birthday party and then we entertained Marion and David from Chesterfield on our wedding anniversary. Another day our former neighbours Jen and Gordon from Wiltshire came to lunch. On June 1st we watched Grace dance in the High School Musical show at Hykeham.

Two weeks later David drove us to Portsmouth for the afternoon ferry to France where Jean and Monique met us. They entertained us like royalty for 10 days, taking us to some of the old haunts and introducing new ones like the lovely gardens at La Colline des Oiseaux near Caen. On a visit to the D-Day Museum at Arromanche, Dick was presented with a plaque after a party of Americans overheard him describing the landings and the terrain. One of them said, "You were here?" and then followed a barrage of questions and the appearance of the curator who took Dick into an office and awarded him the plaque. It was quite an exciting occasion for a man who didn't like a lot of fuss. Later we walked around Courseulles, a pretty coastal resort which was liberated by the Canadians and which has become a favourite resort of ours. It was not far from there that Dick actually landed, at a place called Ver-sur-Mer on 12th June 1944.

Our overnight ferry crossing to Portsmouth was a bit choppy and we returned home by coach. We vowed not to go again without the car but in fact this turned out to be our last visit to Normandy. We had stayed with Jean and Monique 13 times and camped on 23 French campsites.

We were home in time for my niece Jill's 50th birthday party which was a happy occasion, and then Dick's birthday barbeque on a very hot day in the garden with the whole family here.

In August we stayed in a caravan at Downton with David and the girls and spent a lot of time crabbing at Keyhaven and at Mudeford Quay. Favourites like Beaulieu, Lymington, Burley and Exbury Gardens were all on the agenda plus a visit to Southampton by ferry to explore West Quay Shopping Mall. We watched a power boat race from Milford beach and spent an afternoon at the village festival there.

We went back to Downton on our own in October for twelve days and on our way home then spent the last two days in the Chilterns, exploring the beautiful beechwoods and pretty countryside in that area.

In November we joined our village friends on a day's coach trip to Thursford in Norfolk to see the wonderful Christmas Spectacular. There was a new attraction since our last visit, called Fantasy Land, which was fabulous and well worth paying a little extra to see. Christmas was spent with David and we had our usual family lunch together on Boxing Day.

Chapter 41

TO-ING & FRO-ING (2009)

2009 began sadly when Beryl died unexpectedly during the first week. Later in the month we all attended her funeral at Oxford. On February 1st it snowed and carried on for 9 days, falling heavily in some parts of the country and causing chaos on the roads. On the 2nd, London was at a standstill – not even a bus was running! And then 10 days later a rapid thaw caused flooding in many places. I was gifted Beryl's stair lift which was brought from Oxford and fitted for me. It has been a tremendous asset as my mobility has deteriorated.

There was another sad blow to come before the month's end when Tim called to say Mary had died in hospital. We hadn't even known she was ill. Dick had lost his sister and sister-in-law in just two months.

On a happier note, we celebrated my 80th birthday with 15 of us dining at Tom Browns at Gunthorpe. It was a lovely sunny day allowing us to spend some time in our garden to take photos.

Most of March we spent gardening or playing indoor bowls, but by April we were ready for some sea air. First we had 5 days with Barbara at Worthing, enjoying the beautiful spring gardens and countryside in general. Then an overnight stop with Rosemary and Pete, who took us to a nature reserve where there were lots of birds that we don't usually see at home. The highlight of our break was to treat ourselves to two nights at the Avonmouth

Hotel at Mudeford. We had visited on several occasions for coffee or a meal, but we hadn't stayed overnight since 1956 as it was rather expensive. This time we had taken advantage of an offer which was hard to ignore, and it was a fabulous break. We have returned from time to time and are always made welcome.

We returned home to find the garden very colourful and the pear tree a mass of blossom. Many more seeds were sown plus 22 lettuce plants.

In April an X-ray on my back showed that I had scoliosis and a further investigation by MRI scan showed evidence of arthritis there. This had apparently been the cause of much pain in my right hip and pelvis for the last 20 years.

On 9th May we celebrated Eddie's and Luke's birthdays with lunch at the Springfield. An added bonus that morning was that I heard both the cuckoo and the woodpecker. That was not unusual then but would be today, as we rarely hear either bird.

In June we had 10 days at the caravan where we had visits from Rosalind, then Rosemary and Pete when we did some more bird watching. The weather was hot and sunny and we had breakfast on the veranda six days running. We watched the Round the Island yacht race before leaving for home. En route we stopped off at Mottisfont Abbey Gardens to see the roses as this was Rose Week and they were at their very best – I took 24 photos!

There was a lot of rain in July but we picked lots of raspberries and watched Wimbledon. Then we prepared for Dick's 90th birthday. We invited local friends for a drink and snacks in the morning, afternoon or evening. In all 31 people turned up. This was followed by a family barbeque on the Sunday when another 37 visitors arrived. We had a surprise when Ro and Pete's daughter, Lucy and husband Honguk, arrived from South Korea! The rain held off for most of the day but continued through the first week of August.

We set off again for Downton and another caravan, this time with David and Eddie and their families joining us. We had a fabulous week with lots of fun picnics and a day touring the Isle of Wight.

Rosemary and Pete came to stay for a week in September and we visited Chatsworth, Rutland Water and Clumber Park. We saw them again two weeks later when they hired a caravan near ours for Pete's birthday weekend. We had a lovely warm and sunny week there, but it all changed as autumn turned into winter, and we had some extremely cold spells right up until Christmas.

Chapter 42

OUR PROLIFIC VEGETABLE GARDEN (2010)

After the New Year celebrations were over, ice and snow returned to most of the country – the newspapers declaring it 'Frozen Britain'. The temperature fell to -18 degrees in Oxfordshire and -8 degrees at home. 1,000 lorries were stranded on the M3 on the 5th. Things were back to normal by mid-month but an outbreak of Swine Flu meant we had to be inoculated. Not much happened in February so I was able to do some jigsaw puzzles at last.

March and part of April were taken up with planting the vegetable garden and David decorated the sitting room. After Easter it was time for a break, so we had two weeks in the caravan at Downton during which time Rosemary and Pete met us for lunch at Meonstoke to do some reminiscing.

Back home there were more seeds to sow including 67 runner beans! One week later, 52 climbing French beans – we like beans!

In June I began a course of acupuncture as a result of the MRI scan in May. The weather was hot and sunny so we sat in the garden most days and enjoyed the fruits of our gardening days. While watching 'Wimbledon' I noted in my diary that two players had taken their final set to 70-68 in 11 hours and 5 minutes! Phew!

In July David took us to Sally and Masood's wedding at Brighton Pavilion. It was a very colourful occasion with lots of Bangladeshi guests. The following day we drove to Bognor to reminisce and take photos at some memorable spots. We then drove via Meonstoke and on to the Inn at Hawksley for lunch. This was a favourite stop off of David's on his walks with pals around the Hampshire Hangers. After lunch and a brief look at the lovely countryside he showed us Field Marshall Montgomery's grave at Binsted.

Two days at home to mow the lawn, pick French beans, do the washing and packing, and we were off again with David and the girls for 10 days at the caravan. Forty-eight hours later Eddie and Maggie joined us with Emily and Jacob and 2 dogs. In addition to the usual visits to favourite spots we had a day at Poole and a boat ride on the River Avon at Christchurch.

Back at home Lucy and Grace came to stay and we took them to Clumber Park and into Derbyshire, picking up Madge en route for lunch at the Miners Arms – an excellent pub for food where we frequently took Madge and other friends during the summer months.

In September we had an 8-day coach holiday with Highland Heritage staying at the Ben Doran Hotel at Tyndrum. The first outing planned was to the Royal Yacht Britannia at Leith but as we had already been there, we chose to explore the area around Tyndrum on foot.

The next day's outing was the real reason we had booked this holiday - a visit to the Isles of Mull and Iona. But it was a complete washout. It poured with rain from the moment we set off and as we crossed to Mull on the ferry, we could barely see the island. Nor was it any better driving the length of the island to Fionnphort, where we were to take a small boat to Iona, but as we alighted from the coach the wind was driving the rain horizontally into our faces. We hurried to the nearest café and here we stayed for the next 3 hours. About half a dozen hardy souls had decided they were not going to miss out on the visit to Iona and took the ferry across, but afterwards said they wished they hadn't, it was so rough. A few folks sought the nearest pub but the rest of us drank coffee, ate snacks and read the newspapers in this tiny café until the hardy ones returned. The following day was much improved and was spent in Fort William and Fort Augustus in the sunshine. A tour of the Trossachs where we sat by the river at Callender was followed by a visit to Lomond Shores Shopping Centre and the Sealife Centre. Seil Island, Lochgoilhead and Inverary were also on the itinerary, but our last day was a real treat. We were taken to Rothesay on the Isle of Bute where we visited the rather splendid Mount Stuart House with its really beautiful gardens. For me this was a fitting end to yet another wonderful week touring the west of Scotland.

In October we went back to the caravan for 10 days, entertaining Ro and Pete for some bird watching, taking Rosalind out for lunch and visiting Dick's old school friends at Meonstoke. The weather was warm and sunny but with a frost at night so the colours in the New Forest were at their best.

Back home, sadly, at the beginning of November, Pete's ex father–in-law Geoff died suddenly which meant Peter's future in the company took on a whole new role. He had already been with them over 25 years. Geoff had been promoting the British Legion in the run up to Armistice Day, and had all his lorries (about 50) displaying an enormous poppy on the front of each vehicle as they delivered their loads of building materials up and down the country. He had the greatest respect for Dick and his war service with particular emphasis on his award for bravery. So he had invited Dick to his business premises to be photographed with the lorries and a number of Geoff's British Legion friends. It had been planned for the Saturday following Geoff's death and the family insisted that it should go ahead. Fortunately, it was a bright sunny morning which helped lift everyone's spirits and ensured the occasion was accomplished as Geoff would have wished.

The last few days of the month brought several quite heavy falls of snow. The temperature dropped to -18, -17, -10, and -7 on consecutive days and we were housebound for a week. Again the headlines in the press read 'Frozen Britain' as roads, railways and airports were at a standstill. Conditions improved by Christmas and we were able to stay with David as planned. On Christmas Day good news prevailed and we celebrated the arrival of our first great grandchild, Lily Elise, a beautiful baby daughter for Luke and Shara. On Boxing Day 16 of us had lunch at the Old Reindeer at Edingley, and afterwards exchanged presents at David's house which became the norm for the next 8 years.

Chapter 43

THE LAST COACH HOLIDAY OF 35! (2011)

January and February of 2011 were unusually mild and sunny so an early start was made preparing the vegetable garden. We also played a lot of indoor bowls and took Madge for a pub lunch most weeks. In March my friend Rosalind from the New Forest spent a few days at Thoresby Hall. She had for a long time wanted to visit the village of Canwick near Lincoln, where her father had been the vicar when she was young. So we picked her up one morning and entertained her for the day, spending the afternoon around Canwick. Unfortunately the church was locked but a low window enabled us to get a glimpse of the interior and we took lots of photos outside.

On Mothering Sunday we had lunch with Eddie and Maggie at their lovely Victorian house at Lambley. They had worked hard in their garden and I was thrilled to see that Eddie had a sizeable vegetable patch. One of our offspring had become a gardener at last! Soon after this I was dismayed to hear that they were thinking of selling up and moving to Norfolk. They planned to take early retirement from their jobs, and set about restoring a pretty little cottage they had bought in that county. They took us over there one day to show us the area, and it was so lovely I had to support their decision and envied the fact that it was only 20 minutes from the coast. Since then they have restored another bigger cottage in which they are now living. In both cases they gutted the property and re-constructed walls and chimneys, retiled part of the roof, laid new floors and put in all new windows. They have done most of it themselves and worked like Trojans. Eddie is a qualified

225

electrician and self-taught plumber which has proved an asset. Maggie deserves a medal, wheelbarrow-pushing to dispose of tons of rubble.

In May we had what turned out to be our last coach holiday (35 in all), to the Gower Peninsular in South Wales, stopping en route in Evesham for coffee and Abergavenny for lunch, and continuing through the beautiful Wye Valley to our excellent modern hotel at Aberavon Beach near Swansea. This was completely new territory for both of us. As the lanes were so narrow and twisty, we had to take a minibus to explore Rhossili and Worm's Head where we walked for a while. The following day we were treated to a steam train ride through the Brecon Beacons arriving in the smart town of Brecon for the afternoon. The next day we were off to the National Botanic Garden of Wales, where we had booked mobility scooters to take us round the extensive site which was beautifully laid out and very colourful. Later we had time to look at the shops in Carmarthen. On the last day our coach took us to the Mumbles where we had a long walk along the beach, before visiting the Wetland Centre at Llanelli in the afternoon. On our return we were driven through the Forest of Dean and stopped in Gloucester for a while, where we visited the magnificent cathedral and the shops. It had been a packed 6-day trip and most enjoyable.

We then made plans for another visit to the caravan in Hampshire in June, where we had a rare showery week. We pulled in most of our usual visits but we always had Rummikub with us for rainy days. Before leaving, we booked two caravans for a week in August when the family would be joining us. This turned out to be a hot sunny week so we had lots of picnics at our favourite spots as well as lunch at the Christchurch Harbour Hotel.

September was cool and showery and we spent a lot of time picking and freezing hundreds of pears. It seemed as if every bit of that mass of spring blossom had developed into a fruit. They were delicious and kept us going for ages. There were also lots of peas and beans to freeze.

After the usual influx of children at half-term we met David and Marion from Chesterfield at the Miner's Arms in Derbyshire for lunch. It was always a happy occasion as we only usually saw them twice a year.

Nothing of particular interest happened then until Christmas which we spent with David, and the usual get-together for Boxing Day lunch at Edingley when there were 20 of us, followed by a family party at David's house for the opening of presents.

Chapter 44

A NEW GREENHOUSE (2012)

Having cleaned up from our New Year's Eve party I sat and watched the New Year's Day concert from Vienna, which incorporates some spectacular dancing. This has become a regular event which I look forward to, now that Madge no longer comes to stay and we don't go walking. But we still took her out for a pub lunch regularly, and there was always bowls and snooker to watch on TV in January as well as jigsaw puzzles waiting to be done. The month soon disappeared and February ushered in snow and ice and very cold conditions. But later, snowdrops and crocus brought masses of colour to the garden as things warmed up, and March found me in the garden or greenhouse most days. About this time our landlords sent someone to put film on the house windows as a health and safety measure. They had been told to do my greenhouse too but preferred to pull it down and give me a new one – I didn't complain!

The Queen's Diamond Jubilee took place in June on a very wet day. We watched the pageant on the River Thames on TV, and the next day had our own celebration with a picnic at the village hall and a photo taken of all the village community.

On the 13th we set off for the caravan for 10 days and indulged in a much-needed rest.

On our return home we visited the Easton Walled Garden near Grantham to see the wonderful display of sweet peas. It's a garden that has lots to offer at any time of the year.

In July we celebrated Sophie's 21st birthday with dinner at The Lion in Farnsfield. Then David went to Paris for Stephanes 50th surprise birthday party. A week later he drove us south to attend Dominic and Jo's wedding which took place in a huge barn at Kirkford in Sussex. It was a lovely wedding and nice to meet members of the family we hadn't seen for some time. The following day we reminisced at Bognor and Bosham for a while, before driving up to the Cotswolds via Bladon to show David Churchill's grave. We stayed in a lovely B&B we knew near Bourton-on-the-Water and had an excellent evening meal at The Lamb, a delightful old inn at Great Rissington.

In the late evening we wandered round a quiet Bourton, long after the day trippers had gone home. On Sunday, as David didn't know the Cotswolds at all, we showed him several of the very pretty villages, stopping for coffee in Upper Slaughter and lunch in Broadway. He liked the area and vowed to explore it on foot before too long.

As most of the family were away on their various holidays in August, we took a number of friends out for pub lunches at a variety of venues. Then it was time to start picking and freezing produce from the garden and, when most of the fruit and veg had been dealt with, we decided we deserved another break at the caravan. While there we visited Meonstoke and were told that, sadly, Dick's old school friend Ted had died the previous October. We also met up with our old neighbours Jen and Gordon for lunch at Burley, but service was so slow that we had to leave early to meet their grandchildren from school. So we finished up at the Potting Shed café for pudding along with the children, and then back to Jo's house for tea.
39
In October Lily was christened at Bottesford Church followed by a large gathering for Sunday lunch at the village hall there. November was frosty and foggy and we had floods, and a repeat performance of all three in December.

The year ended with Christmas at David's and the usual Boxing Day lunch at Edingley for 20 of us. We were entertained by our friends Jean and Frank to a superb New Year's Eve meal followed by Rummikub well into the early hours of 2013.

Chapter 45

LAST VISIT TO THE CARAVAN (2013)

I took advantage of a fairly mild and sunny New Year to tidy up the garden, but by the middle of the month it turned cold and icy and we had several falls of snow. Every morning we had a very welcome visitor – a goldcrest busied itself searching for insects and seeds in the pine tree outside our bedroom window. We watched him regularly while we had our early morning cup of tea! They are quite tiny birds, the smallest of our native breeds. February provided a mixture of cold winds and warm sunny days.

March was again cold and windy with heavy snow in places and drifts blocking roads in Scotland and the north-west. The cold weather carried on well into April so gardening was confined to the greenhouse. On the 6th April we clocked up 55 years at Rolleston. Not until the 29th did it begin to warm up and some lovely sunny days brought out the plum and cherry blossom and the magnolia stellata. The gardening got into full swing and the cuckoo was heard on several occasions.

We celebrated Emily's 21st birthday at the end of May and two days later set off for the caravan. We were ready for a breath of sea air! But it didn't do us much good. After a few very hot days we both developed a cough and Dick wasn't well, so we came home and disappointingly we never got the chance to return.

Our next event was Ruth and Victor's Golden Wedding celebration lunch at the Cotgrave Country Club. Dick's cousin Ruth was married to Victor, a Sierra-Leonian with Nigerian ancestors. Following visits there in recent years, he had discovered that he was a Prince by birth and had been invited back to his native country to have the title bestowed on him. At the celebrations we were attending, Victor and Ruth were dressed in their very colourful robes as Prince Nwa and Princess Nwami. A lot of the guests were African, all dressed and bejewelled in their traditional finery. It was a wonderful and very happy occasion.

A few days later we were celebrating again – this time Maggie's 50th birthday – with dinner at the Magna Charta at Lowdham. Then a few days later we celebrated Dick's 94th birthday at the Nags Head in Woodborough. For two weeks it had been extremely hot - up to 31 degrees – and we badly needed rain. Eventually it arrived, but too much of it and thunderstorms, which brought flooding to Southwell where 100 homes were affected and parked cars were floating. 67.8mm were recorded in 30 minutes.

After several days of torrential downpours the rain stopped, and the sun came out on the day of Matthew and Sammy-Jo's wedding. They were married at Bottesford Church and we were able to take lots of photos in the pretty churchyard. The reception was Sunday lunch in the village hall there, followed by a disco in the evening.

In August we had quite a few casual visitors and we took friends out to lunch. Then in September and October it was business as usual with the preparation and freezing of apples, pears, plums, beans and peas. We were inundated with them, which was great! Nothing very exciting happened for the rest of the year, except for a day in Derbyshire with our friends David and Marion from Chesterfield which we always enjoyed. We were with David for Christmas as usual, with our Boxing Day family lunch at the White Post this year. We entertained our friends to dinner on the 31st and several games of Rummikub propelled us into the New Year.

Chapter 46

WATER, WATER EVERYWHERE (2014)

News of the arrival of Matthew Peter to Matt and Sammy-Jo on the 4th January started our New Year.

Throughout January and February there was extensive flooding in the south-west, particularly the Somerset Levels. We read in the press that shingle from the beaches at Milford-on-Sea had been thrown, by the heavy swells, through the windows of a sea front hotel sending evening diners scurrying to safety. This was very near to where our caravan had been. In Nottinghamshire we got off lightly, just losing the roof of our old pigsty in a gale.

For a few weeks I was compelled to slow down in the garden, having hurt my right wrist pruning shrubs, so I sat outside with my arm in a sling and enjoyed the fruits of my labour. At the beginning of June we watched the 70th D-Day celebrations in Normandy on TV. David saw part of it en route to our friend Jean's 80th birthday party at Cahagnes.

By the second half of July the weather had become very hot and on the last Sunday, when we celebrated Dick's 95th birthday with our usual barbeque, the children were able to enjoy the paddling pool as well as Thomas the Tank Engine which Dick had built for them some years earlier.

We hadn't had a holiday so Eddie and Maggie fetched us to stay with them in Norfolk for a few days. The cottage they had restored was delightful. They had done almost all the work themselves and had worked hard. They took us to many of the pretty coastal villages such as Cley, Salthouse, Blakeney and Holkham where we watched the boats and birds. At Burnham Overy Staithe I recognised the cottage I had shared with my art friends a few years earlier.

We sampled some of their favourite eateries and had fish and chips sitting on the sea wall at Wells-next-the-Sea, a must do event it seems, for everyone who knows the area!

Luke and Shara's wedding day dawned on the 2nd October but I had a rude awakening! At 5am I found the bathroom floor flooded and water pouring from a tap whose washer had given up. On investigating downstairs, I discovered it dripping through the kitchen ceiling on to the cooker and the fridge with some water already on the floor. Neither Dick or I could manage to close the stop tap and were obliged to rouse our ever-willing neighbours, Gayle and Mike, who lived opposite. I was very distressed as I thought we should miss the wedding but our valiant neighbours took over and insisted we must go. When we returned everything was clean and dry and they had even found a plumber to come and renew the offending washer! We shall never forget their kindness and hard work.

Unfortunately the weather for the wedding was as wet as our bathroom floor had been, so we were unable to take outdoor photos. The church porch at Bottesford filled with umbrellas as we entered for a lovely wedding, followed by a superb reception at a nearby hotel. Later that month there was an engagement party for Sophie and Damian in Southwell heralding another family marriage in the not-too-distant future.

In November Dick was invited to talk to 10-year-old pupils, at the school where Sophie was teaching in Mansfield, about his experiences in the Second World War. We took along lots of memorabilia including two large scrapbooks of photos and newspaper cuttings which we had previously put together. The children showed extreme interest and asked lots of intelligent questions. As I had been their age at the beginning of the war, they were also keen to know how it had affected me and my family at home in Nottingham. It was a most stimulating encounter with these youngsters.

Fast forward to Christmas and we stayed for 2 nights with David. His family joined us on the 25th and then, on Boxing Day, the whole family (21 of us) had lunch at the Old Reindeer at Edingley as usual. Everyone returned to David's house to open presents and we were all so preoccupied in this ritual, that it was much later when Alfie noticed it was snowing very heavily and apparently had been doing for some time. This was a little alarming as many of the family had some distance to travel home. They packed up and departed promptly and all had problems en route, but ironically Sophie and Damian, who lived only four miles away, struggled for three hours before abandoning the car and completing their journey on foot.

David took us home the next morning on very icy roads, only to find that our central heating had broken down and the house was cold. We called our insurance company and heating engineer but no-one was available for 2 days. We returned to David's and there we stayed for three whole weeks, returning home most days to meet engineers who seemed to be having tremendous problems. In the end on the 16th January the landlord condemned the boiler and a new one was installed. At last we had a warm home to return to. What a start to 2015!

Chapter 47

CELEBRATIONS, THEN A BOMBSHELL (2015)

There was a lot of snow in many parts of the country during January and on the 28th we had a minor earthquake (3.8) centred in the Leicestershire town of Oakham.

February was considerably warmer with some lovely sunny days, made even brighter by David giving the kitchen a fresh coat of paint.

In March and April we were busy in the garden sowing and planting. Sadly we said goodbye to Marigold after a short illness. In May we celebrated our Diamond Wedding, first with a dinner party that evening at the Boathouse at Farndon, and the next day we partied again at the village coffee morning. But the 'biggy' came later in the month when 50 guests enjoyed Sunday lunch at The Nottinghamshire, formerly Cotgrave Golf and Country Club. It was a truly wonderful occasion in a wonderful setting and almost all our relations and friends were able to come.

A different type of celebration took place one evening when we were invited to Lucy's graduation at Mansfield College, following her catering and hospitality course. We were served a seven-course meal by the students which they had prepared and cooked themselves. It was fabulous!

Having watched Ascot and Wimbledon on TV it was time to start picking raspberries and currants which kept us busy for several weeks.

On Dick's 96th birthday Rosemary and Pete came for a few days and took us to Clumber Park, pushing us round in wheelchairs. We had lunch at our favourite School House at Carburton and tea with Louise on the way home. Our annual barbeque took place on the Sunday but it rained heavily all afternoon, so the boys cooked under a gazebo and parasols, and 18 of us crammed into our sun lounge balancing plates on our knees.

For the next two months nothing very exciting happened. We were both beginning to slow down. Apart from the odd lunch out with friends, Dick preferred to stay at home and indulge in his new-found hobby of jigsaw puzzles. He became very adept at them and was clocking up 3 x 1000-piece jigsaws about every two weeks. The arthritis in my back became worse so Maggie and her sister Julie came on lots of occasions to help with the gardening.

Then in October we received a bombshell! Our landlords, Notts County Council, were planning to sell the smallholding which we rented. We knew we couldn't afford to buy it and our boys had all recently spent large sums improving their own homes. We were devastated. Thinking we should have to vacate the property we hired a skip and began de-cluttering.
Early in November estate agents came to value the property and a sale/auction board went up. We had no idea where we should go or when, but the landlord was compelled to re-house us. The worry made us both quite ill and we seemed to be constantly visiting the nurse to have our blood pressure checked.

Christmas came and went; the usual family gatherings having taken place, and on New Year's Day 2016 things began to look up and heralded in a better year than we had anticipated.

Chapter 48

TWO WEDDINGS & MUCH REJOICING (2016)

Pete and Kate took us to lunch at Washingborough Hall near Lincoln, where they were planning to hold their wedding reception on Easter Saturday. We had an excellent meal and agreed it would be an ideal venue for their special day.

But first we had to survive some inconvenience in February and March, from estate agents taking photos inside the house as well as out, and then a block viewing day with all and sundry traipsing through our dwelling, many being inquisitive rather than potential buyers. It was horrible! When the day of the auction arrived, the three boys and other family members went to Nottingham Racecourse to witness it. Imagine our surprise and elation when they rang to say someone in our family had bought the property so that Dick and I could remain in it as tenants. How we rejoiced! We couldn't thank them enough. Now we could relax and look forward to Pete and Kate's wedding in a few days' time.

They were married at All Saints' Church in Collingham and then we took over Washingborough Hall for the rest of the day and night, as several family members stayed over until Easter Sunday. The whole occasion was greatly enjoyed by about 60 guests.

Not a great deal of interest happened until July when we celebrated another family wedding, that of Sophie and Damian (Dink to most people). This took place at St. Michael's Church in Farnsfield on a beautiful hot summer's day.

After a lovely service and a lot of photos afterwards, the couple left in a white vintage car for the reception at Norwood Hall in Southwell. Here we sat out on the lawns and took photos by a magnificent lavender hedge. After an excellent meal the youngsters danced the night away while we slept for the night in this lovely old country house.

The next day there was yet more partying as Victor celebrated his 80th birthday at The Nottinghamshire. It turned out to be an exceptionally hot week, the temperature reaching 90 degrees F on four days.

Rosemary and Pete brought Lucy and her two little girls, Hannah and Genna from South Korea, to see us. We sat in the shade eating ice creams. That day Emily's baby Noah was born. On the following Sunday we celebrated Dick's 97th birthday with a barbeque for 16 of us.

The family went off on their various holidays but we stayed at home, enjoying the odd day out in Derbyshire and some pub meals with friends. There was excitement in November when Dick was awarded the French Légion d'honneur. He chose not to travel to Birmingham to have it presented so it arrived by post! The local press came to take a photo of him wearing the medal and an article about his war service appeared along with it.

One more family gathering happened in December for Noah's christening at the Holy Trinity Church in Southwell, followed by a party at Southwell Rugby Club. We spent Christmas with David as usual and once again the whole family enjoyed Boxing Day lunch at the Old Reindeer at Edingley.

Eddie retired from Network Rail at the end of the year to concentrate on refurbishing another cottage in Norfolk. Our New Year celebrations had to be cancelled as Dick had a chest infection and spent 24 hours in hospital.

Chapter 49

A NASTY ACCIDENT (2017)

At the beginning of February Eddie and Maggie sold their house at Lowdham and went to live in Norfolk permanently.

Lucy flew to New Zealand on her own to join friends who were backpacking. We received photos from her skydiving! My diary tells me I saw the sunrise three times that week. Early in April my nephew Nigel had an accident and sadly died three days later. Apparently he had a heart attack. The same day Dick's cousin Ruth died – not a happy time.

In July we celebrated Noah's 1st birthday followed by the usual family barbeque for Dick's 98th birthday.

It was about this time that I realised I must get on with writing my memoirs, so out came my diaries from 1964 onwards and hundreds of photos taken throughout my life. My father had always taken lots of 'snaps' and some were very old sepia ones. I had a wonderful time reminiscing.

At the beginning of September we were invited to Tony and Sharon's Ruby Wedding celebration at Newmarket, so we made a weekend of it. First David took us to Docking in Norfolk to have lunch at the first cottage Eddie and Maggie had restored and where they were living. Then on to Binham, a little nearer the coast, where work was still very much in progress on the second cottage. They have worked tremendously hard and turned it into a beautiful home. We all had a meal at the local pub and then David drove us to Newmarket where we had booked two nights at a Premier Inn. On the Sunday the celebration was held in a local village hall where Tony and Sharon, with the help of a few friends, had provided a very substantial and most enjoyable meal for all their family and friends.

The party continued at their lovely home overlooking the Gallops, which had been the original Newmarket racecourse. We returned to the hotel for the night but were invited back to their house for breakfast next morning before setting off for home.

Sadly that turned out to be our last short break together, as in October Dick had a bizarre accident. We had had coffee at our village hall as usual on a Wednesday, and as Dick got into the car his left foot slipped on a patch of mud and he broke his ankle on the edge of the car. It was a bad open break and bled profusely so an ambulance was summoned. As he was taking blood thinning medication, they alerted the Air Ambulance which had only recently begun carrying blood supplies. Imagine my surprise and relief when the helicopter flew in. In fact Dick was taken to hospital by road, accompanied by the Air Ambulance doctor with his box of blood. The ankle was operated on the next day and healed well. He came home briefly in November but we both developed a chest infection. Dick was re-admitted to hospital and I spent a few days in bed. After 3 months in various hospitals he was discharged. Carers came 4 times a day but by mid-February it was clear he needed full time care and went into a care home in Newark.

Heavy snow and blizzards at the beginning of March were so cold that they were named 'The Beast from the East'. We had difficulty getting about but made sure Dick had a visitor every day. I was exhausted and my arthritis worsened so I had to be content to keep warm and watch the Winter Olympics on TV. Several of the family came to see me on my birthday and a few days later I had a surprise visit from Ro and Pete from Sussex and Tony and Sharon from Newmarket. On Easter Sunday David fetched me to have lunch with him and Lucy, and on Monday Eddie and Jacob spent the day with me and cooked the dinner. The weather remained very cold but the gardener managed to mow the lawns for the first time.

I had a day out with Luke, Shara and Lily when they took me to the Blue Diamond Garden Centre for lunch and a good look round and then went on to visit Dick. It was clear he was beginning to deteriorate. The ankle had healed but the accident and the six months spent in bed had taken its toll on his vital organs

Chapter 50

FAREWELL TO MY DEAR HUSBAND (2018)

Dick spent three months in various hospitals and then came home at the beginning of February. After a fortnight at home I just couldn't cope even with the help of carers and he went into a care home. I was so exhausted I slept for a week apart from visiting him every evening. He died in May just a few weeks before his 99th birthday. He had done very well and lived a very full life. There were 101 people at his funeral service. He had made friends everywhere he went. He was Richard to his family and Dick among the farming community and of course 'Curly' to his army comrades.

I had never lived alone so now I have had to re-adjust – we had been married for 3 days short of 63 years and been very happy. Our three sons and their families have been extremely good to me and afforded me a lot of their time, so I am not lonely and not bored because I have so many interests. I still have my lovely garden, but arthritis prevents me from tending it – instead two very able gardeners keep it in trim and quite colourful. Most of all I miss growing my own vegetables.

Dick had commented that he would like his ashes to be scattered on the River Meon in Hampshire where he had spent a very happy childhood. So in July Pete and family and David and I met there for this purpose and spent the weekend enjoying the area and visiting Dick's old school and his early family home.

In August Eddie and Maggie came for a weekend and did lots of small jobs, took me out for lunch and picked lots of apples and plums.

I had decided that I must support the Air Ambulance as they had come when Dick had his accident and they rely on charity alone. So I had a good turn out and sent half a van load which they collected for their various shops. Later in the month Peter supported their 'Ride to Save Lives' 70-mile motorcycle run from Newark Showground. I was taken to see the start and finish which was quite spectacular as hundreds of bikes took part.

In November David decided I needed a break, so on the 18th he took me south to Mudeford to the lovely Christchurch Harbour Hotel. We went via my favourite country route, stopping off for coffee and then lunch. We spent two full days visiting our favourite spots from our caravan days and then we came home via the Cotswolds, another greatly loved area of mine, stopping off in the charming village of Great Rissington for a pub lunch. The next day I became the proud owner of a nearly new Honda Jazz – a comfy little car, not quite as majestic as the trusty Mercedes I had owned for 12 years.

Very sadly on December 20th my friend for 86 years, Madge, died. We had some wonderful times together as children growing up, as teenagers on holiday together, not to mention hours and hours on the local tennis courts. Her parents had treated me like another daughter after the death of my mother and had entertained me tirelessly. Madge had lost her husband Don in his 40s so spent a lot of her life in our company, not having family of her own - I miss her greatly.

I spent Christmas at David's and we had the usual family Boxing Day lunch for the whole family (20 of us) at the Old Reindeer at Edingley.

Chapter 51

ON REACHING '90' (2019)

The New Year began with the arrival on January 4th of baby Harriet to Sophie and Damian, and first grandchild for David. By the 10th the mild weather provided a show of early snowdrops and, apart from the odd frost, most of February remained mild and sunny and I was able to sit in the sun lounge most days.

For my 90th birthday in March the family took me to the The Nottinghamshire for Sunday lunch. They included Tony and Sharon and Rosemary and Pete in the party. We had a wonderful celebration. Eddie and Maggie came back for the weekend two weeks later, and all three boys took down the large Christmas tree near the front door as it was 50% dead and taller than the house – a mammoth task.

On Mothering Sunday Pete and his family took me to The Boathouse at Farndon for lunch.

In April I had a surprise visit from Helen who had been the Cub Leader at Farndon when I was the Scout Leader. We did a lot of reminiscing!

In May I lost two very close friends, Norman who had previously been our vicar for several years, and Marion at Chesterfield who I met in 1948/9. I had been her bridesmaid and her husband David had married us.

For my birthday I was given tickets to Chatsworth Flower Show in June, a spectacular annual event which I had longed to visit. Peter took me along with my friend Amanda and we had a really enjoyable day and of course, bought some plants!

The last week of the month Sophie, Damian and Harriet were holidaying in a caravan at Milford-on-Sea, so David took me down for 4 days to the Christchurch Harbour Hotel at Mudeford. We joined the family for some of the time and explored the old haunts, taking lots of photos of the four generations together.

At the end of June my dear friend Joyce Todd died, just two months after her husband Norman.

Eddie and Maggie came for a weekend in July and took me to the Easton Walled Garden near Grantham to see the spectacular display of sweet peas. It was a fabulous day out for me. Then I settled down to watch 'Wimbledon' on TV. At the end of the month, we had our annual family barbeque to celebrate what would have been Dick's 100th birthday. Tony and Sharon joined us and Ro and Pete brought Sally and Lana with them. There were 30 people here, 8 of them children who had a wonderful afternoon riding on the garden trailer and on Thomas the Tank Engine.

About this time my right knee became very painful with arthritis so I didn't go far – not being able to walk or stand without discomfort. I tried all kinds of painkillers but nothing took away the pain. I had lots of visits from family and friends and some took me out to lunch, and then there was the Christmas Fuddle at the village hall. But the highlight of the pre-Christmas period was David's 60th birthday party also at the village hall. There were about 60 guests from far and wide, Stephane bringing his family from Paris. They stayed with David overnight and then spent Sunday morning with me, making it a very enjoyable weekend. Sophie invited me to join them for Christmas dinner which Damian cooked, making a most professional job of it.

As David no longer lived in Farnsfield, we decided to meet up for our family Boxing Day lunch at the Royal Oak at Collingham, and then invaded Pete and Kate's home for the grand present opening and tea and cakes. That concluded our normal family and no-one could have foreseen what lay ahead in the year 2020.

Chapter 52

A BRIEF ENCOUNTER THEN 'LOCKDOWN' (2020)

It began well enough for the first two months. In February David and I attended a Gang Show Reunion at Newark Showground, where we met up with many ex-scouting comrades who had taken part in several Gang Shows at Newark Palace Theatre in the 1970s, some as Scouts and others as Leaders. Now some Leaders were in wheelchairs, like me and Scouts had grown up and become Leaders. It was an exhilarating experience as we sang "We're riding along on the crest of a wave". But none of us knew quite where that wave was taking us in the coming months!

Our final family gathering at the beginning of March was to celebrate my 91st birthday with Sunday lunch at Southwell's Hearty Good Fellow pub. The next day I drove my car to Southwell for the very last time. It was a sad day for me as I had really enjoyed driving both in this country and abroad for 70 years.

Then came the Coronavirus pandemic and by 23rd the whole country was in 'lockdown'. I shall now leave the outcome for some other diarist to relate.

Historical Notes

Communication.

Before the Second World War letters cost 1d (penny) and a postcard 1/2d (halfpenny) in old money and there were two deliveries a day – early morning and early afternoon. Telegrams brought urgent messages or greetings and were delivered by a boy on a red bicycle. Parcels were wrapped in brown paper and tied with string. There was no Sellotape or plastic of any kind. Red sealing wax was used on large or important parcels.

We had newspapers and wireless but no TV, and very few private houses had a telephone and certainly no mobile phones. There was a half-mile walk to the nearest telephone box so there could be considerable delay if a doctor or the fire brigade were required. Most policemen were on foot or on bicycles – no cars with sirens. There were few traffic lights but at busy junctions a policeman stood on a box on 'point duty' directing the traffic. Ambulances rang a single bell, fire engines a jangle of bells. There were no motorways or ring roads until well after the War

Transport.

Buses, trams and trolleybuses were in regular use as were many local steam trains. Taxis were available but expensive. A lot of people used bicycles and motorcycles but people tended to walk everywhere.

Household.

Spring Cleaning was an annual ritual when the whole house was 'turned out'. Carpets (not many fitted) were taken up and beaten outside with a beater resembling a large willow tennis racket. Painting and wallpapering were done, curtains washed and all wooden items and silver and brass polished.

We even had some dinner knives whose blades required cleaning with some kind of paste on a cork. Not a favourite job!

On Washday (Monday, except on bank Holiday) the copper in the kitchen would be filled and brought to the boil. There bed linen, towels and other white items would be boiled with soap powder.

Other items were put in a dolly tub and would be twisted and turned with 'dolly pegs'. More delicate items were ponched with a 'poncher' – something resembling an upside-down colander on a long handle. To rinse, these procedures took place at least twice more with clear water. Then began the really hard work, everything was put through the mangle, which was a heavy iron object with heavy wooden rollers through which every item passed as the heavy handle was turned. Everything was then pegged out on the clothes line in the garden unless of course it was raining – then it hung in front of the fire on a 'clothes horse'.

The rest of Monday and part of Tuesday was spent ironing. A flat iron stood on a trivet by the fire to heat up. Eventually electric irons became available, but there were no washing machines or dryers until sometime after the war. Very few houses had central heating. Almost every room had an open fireplace for burning coal or logs. The ashes had to be cleared out each morning when they had cooled. Chimneys were swept twice a year by a regular chimney sweep.

There was no double glazing so houses generally were much colder. Everyone wore more clothes and warmer ones, like woollen vests and woollen stockings. There was frequently ice on the <u>inside</u> of the windows in winter.

Large old houses often had a coal-fired cooking range kept clean with black lead polish – a dirty job. A black iron kettle stood on the hob all day.

Food.

There were no fridges or freezers in private homes before the war. Everyone had a pantry (or larder) with a concrete bench for fresh food. A small window for ventilation would be covered with mesh to keep out flies but if one got in through the door, we might find maggots in our breakfast bacon!

Milk was delivered daily, but if some did turn sour we made soft cheese by straining in through muslin and adding a small amount of salt. Because most housewives didn't go out to work, they would shop most days for fresh food, except Sundays and Bank Holidays when all shops were closed. If bread went stale, we toasted it by the glowing embers of the fire on the end of a long handled toasting fork.

Printed in Great Britain
by Amazon

29102445R00145